How to CONDUCT SURVEYS

A Step-by-Step Guide

Arlene Fink

SAGE Publications
Thousand Oaks ■ London ■ New Delhi

For information:

Sage Publications, Inc.
2455 Teller Road
Thousand Oaks, California 91320
E-mail: order@sagepub.com

Sage Publications Ltd.
1 Oliver's Yard
55 City Road
London EC1Y 1SP
United Kingdom

Sage Publications India Pvt. Ltd.
B-42, Panchsheel Enclave
Post Box 4109
New Delhi 110 017 India

Printed in the United States of America

Library of Congress Cataloging-in-Publication Data

Fink, Arlene.
How to conduct surveys: A step-by-step guide / Arlene Fink.—3rd ed.
    p. cm.
Includes bibliographical references and index.
ISBN 1-4129-1423-X (pbk.)
    1. Social surveys. 2. Educational surveys. I. Title.
HN29.F53 2006
300′.72′3—dc22   2005002435

This book is printed on acid-free paper.

06   07   08   09   8   7   6   5   4   3   2

Acquisitions Editor:	Lisa Cuevas Shaw
Editorial Assistant:	Karen Wong
Production Editor:	Diane S. Foster
Copy Editor:	Linda Gray
Typesetter:	C&M Digitals (P) Ltd.
Proofreader:	Mary Meagher
Indexer:	Judy Hunt
Cover Designer:	Glenn Vogel

THIRD EDITION

How to CONDUCT SURVEYS

WITHDRAWN

7 Day Loan

*This book is dedicated to the ones
I love: John C. Beck, Astrid, and Daniella*

CONTENTS

Preface   ix

1. **Conducting Surveys: Everyone Is Doing It**   **1**
   Overview   1
   What Is a Survey?   1
   When Is a Survey Best?   3
   Questionnaires and Interviews: The Heart of the Matter   4
   Survey Types: The Friendly Competition   7
   A Survey Continuum: From Specific to General Use   8

2. **The Survey Form: Questions, Scales, and Appearance**   **11**
   Overview   11
   The Content Is the Message   12
   Define the Terms   12
   Select Your Information Needs or Hypotheses   12
   Make Sure You Can Get the Information Needed   13
   Do Not Ask for Information Unless You Can Act on It   13
   Writing Questions   13
   Organizing Responses to Open-Ended Survey Items:
       Do You Get Any Satisfaction?   15
   Rules for Writing Closed Survey Questions   18
   Responses for Closed Questions   21
   Rating Scales   23

3. **Getting It Together: Some Practical Concerns**   **31**
   Overview   31
   Length   32
   Putting Questions in Order   32
   Questionnaire Format: Aesthetics and Other Concerns   34
   Branching Questions, or the Infamous "Skip" Pattern   34
   Administration   35
   The Survey Is Put on Trial   37
   Guidelines for Pilot Testing   40
   Ethics, Privacy, and Confidentiality   41
   A Far-Reaching World: Surveys, Language, and Culture   43

4. **Sampling**   **45**
   Overview   45
   Sample Size and Response Rate: Who and How Many?   46

Probability Sampling Methods 47
Nonprobability Sampling Methods 50
Finding the Sample 51
How Large Should Your Sample Be? 52
Response Rate 57

5. **Survey Design: Environmental Control** **59**
Overview 59
Which Designs Are Available? 60
Cross-Sectional Survey Designs 60
Longitudinal Surveys 62
Cohort Designs 63
Panel Designs 63
Comparison Group Survey Designs: Quasi- and True Experiments 64
Other Survey Designs: Normative and Case Control 66

6. **Analyzing and Organizing Data From Surveys** **69**
Overview 69
What Is Typical Anyway? Some Commonly
Used Methods for Analyzing Survey Data 70
Putting the Horse in Front of the Cart: Selecting Analysis Methods 73
Statistical Significance 76
A Technical Interlude 77
Data Organization or Management 85
Creating a Code Book 85

7. **Presenting the Survey Results** **91**
Overview 91
Reproducing the Questionnaire 91
Using Tables 92
Drawing Pie Diagrams 93
Using Bar Graphs 94
Using Line Graphs 95
Drawing Diagrams or Pictures 95
Writing the Results of a Survey 96
The Oral Presentation 99
Computerized "Slide" Presentations 99
Oral Versus Written Reports: A Difference in Conversation 100

Bibliography **103**

Index **105**

About the Author **109**

PREFACE

T he third edition of this book shares the same goal as the first and second: to guide readers in developing their own rigorous surveys and evaluating the credibility of other ones. Like the first and second editions, this one also gives practical step-by-step advice on how to achieve the goal. But most of the similarities end here.

We have completely revised this edition to reflect changes in the way people prepare surveys, use them with the public, and report the results. You will find that this book now covers computer-assisted and interactive surveys. We ask and answer questions such as, How do computer-based and online surveys compare in uses, outcomes, and costs with more traditional survey methods such as telephone interviews and mailed questionnaires? Does new technology mean better surveys? We also discuss methods of ensuring that the survey sample you plan to assemble—regardless of type of survey— will be large enough to detect a difference between groups (if one exists).

Surveys, which are used in nearly every setting from business to the arts, have come under increasing scrutiny for possible violations of privacy. To help you with that hurdle, this third edition provides guidelines for preparing informed consent statements for survey respondents and for asking them sensitive questions about ethnicity, income, and gender. In recent years, we have also recognized the need for translating surveys—even small ones—into other languages, and this edition of the book provides step-by-step advice on how to ensure that your translation gets you the information you need.

Survey research has undergone important changes since the publication of the second edition of this book. First, we have come to rely almost totally on computers to organize and manage survey data (even in very small surveys). Even though we still provide survey results in written reports, we also use presentation software to give them orally. Another change is that surveyors have had to learn even more about privacy than they had to know previously and to pay attention to human subjects' protection. This is not surprising in that e-mail and online surveys have become routine, and with their introduction, surveyors have had to come to terms with new methods of ensuring privacy.

In light of these changes, the third edition has added these new objectives:
The reader will learn how to do the following:

- Create a code book
- Establish the reliability of the coding
- Recognize techniques for dealing with incomplete or missing data and outliers and for recoding
- Identify methods for entering accurate data into spreadsheets, database management programs, and statistical programs

- Prepare a computer presentation (e.g., using PowerPoint)
- Deliver the presentation to an audience
- Use standard ethical principles in guiding survey development
- Describe the main components of an informed consent form
- Distinguish between privacy and confidentiality
- Prepare Web survey questions, including those with dropdown lists, check all that apply, and open-ended questions

We have also updated the examples and references.

We have geared the book for everyone who needs to learn how to do a survey regardless of statistical background. We think the book is useful for self-learning and in workshops, seminars, and formal classrooms.

1

CONDUCTING SURVEYS

Everyone Is Doing It

OVERVIEW

Surveys are used to collect information from or about people to describe, compare, or explain their knowledge, feelings, values, and behavior. Surveys typically take the form of self-administered questionnaires and interviews. Self-administered questionnaires can be completed by hand ("paper-and-pencil" or touch screen) or by computer (on- or offline). Interviews may take place in person ("face-to-face"), on the telephone, or via teleconference. Survey data are used by program planners, evaluators, researchers, and policy leaders in diverse fields, including business, health, social welfare, and politics.

Surveyors must decide on the survey's overall purposes and specific questions. They also need to know who and how many people will be contacted (sampling) and when and how often the survey will take place (design). Surveyors must also process, analyze, and interpret data.

To choose among survey types (self-administered questionnaires or interviews) or methods of administration (mail, telephone, or computer), you need to select one that will produce credible and accurate results and for which you have resources.

Survey purposes and methods fall on a continuum. Some surveys can have far-reaching, generalizable effects, and their methods must be scientific. Surveys of the population's health conducted by the U.S. government are examples of scientific surveys. Other surveys are conducted to meet very specific needs; their methods may not always achieve the highest standards of scientific rigor, but they must still produce accurate results and so must use reliable and valid techniques. Polling students in a particular school to identify their summer reading choices so as to be sure the library is well-stocked is an illustration of a survey designed to meet a specific need.

WHAT IS A SURVEY?

Surveys are information collection methods used to describe, compare, or explain individual and societal knowledge, feelings, values, preferences, and behavior. A survey can be a self-administered questionnaire that someone fills out alone or with assistance. Or a survey can be an interview done in person, on the telephone, or via teleconference. Some surveys are on paper or online and the respondent can complete them privately at home or in a central location—say, at a health center.

The respondent can either return the completed survey by snail mail, e-mail, or online. Surveys can also be interactive and guide the respondent through the questions. Interactive surveys also may provide audio and visual cues to help.

Here at least three good reasons for conducting surveys:

Reason 1: A policy needs to be set or a program must be planned.

Examples: Surveys to Meet Policy or Program Needs

- The YMC Corporation wants to determine which hours to be open each day. The Corporation surveys employees to find out which eight-hour shifts they are willing to work.
- The national office of the Health Voluntary Agency is considering providing day care for its children's staff. How many have very young children? How many would use the Agency's facility?
- Ten years ago, the Bartley School District changed its language arts curriculum. Since then, some people have argued that the curriculum has become out of date. What do the English teachers think? If revisions are needed, what should they look like?

Reason 2: You want to evaluate the effectiveness of programs to change people's knowledge, attitudes, health, or welfare.

Examples: Surveys in Evaluations of Programs

- The YMC Corporation has created two programs to educate people about the advantages and disadvantages of working at unusual hours. One program takes the form of individual counseling and specially prepared, self-monitored videotape. The second program is conducted in large groups. A survey is conducted six months after each program is completed to find out if the employees think they got the information they needed. The survey also aims to find out if they would recommend that others participate in a similar program and how satisfied they are with their work schedule.
- The Health Voluntary Agency is trying two approaches to child care. One is primarily "child centered," and the children usually decide from a list of activities which ones they would like to do during the hours they are in the program. The other is academic and artistic. Children are taught to read, play musical instruments, and dance at set times during the day. Which program is most satisfactory in that the parents, children, and staff are active participants and pleased with the curriculum's content?
- The Bartley School District changed its language arts curriculum. A survey is conducted to find out whether and how the change has affected parents' and students' opinions of the high school program.

Reason 3: You are a researcher and a survey is used to assist you.

Examples: Surveys for Research

- Because the YMC Corporation has so many educational programs, they want to research how adults learn best. Do they prefer self-learning or formal classes? Are reading materials appropriate or are films and videotapes better? How do they feel about computer-assisted learning or learning directly from the Internet? As part of their research, and to make sure all the possibilities are covered, the Corporation conducts a survey of a sample of employees to learn their preferences.
- The Health Voluntary Agency is considering joining with a local university in a study of preschool education. The Agency conducts a survey of the parents participating in the new day care programs. The survey asks about the participants' education and income. Researchers need data such as these so that they can test one of their major assumptions—namely, that parents with higher education and incomes are more likely to choose the more academic of the two preschool programs.
- The Bartley School District is part of a federally funded national study of the teaching of the English language. The study's researchers hypothesized that classroom teaching depends more on their teachers' educational backgrounds and reading preferences than on the formal curriculum. A survey is conducted to find out teachers' educational backgrounds and reading habits so that those data are available for testing the researchers' hypothesis.

WHEN IS A SURVEY BEST?

Many methods are available for obtaining information about people. A survey is only one. Consider the youth center that has as its major aim to provide a variety of services to the community. It offers medical, financial, legal, and educational assistance to residents of the city who are between 12 and 21 years of age regardless of economic or ethnic background. The program is particularly proud of its coordinated approach, arguing that the center's effectiveness comes from making available many services in one location to all participants. Now that the center is ten years old, a survey is to be conducted to find out just how successful it really is. Are participants and staff satisfied? What services do young people use? Is the center really a multiservice one? Are people better off with their health and other needs because of their participation in the center? A mailed self-administered questionnaire survey is decided on to help answer these and other questions. Here are some excerpts from the questionnaire:

Examples: From an Overly Ambitious Self-Administered Questionnaire

5. Is your blood pressure now normal? _11_
    Yes   1
    No   2

7. Which of the following social services have you used in the last 12 months? (Please indicate yes or no for each service.) _15–18_

Services	Yes	No
Medical	1	2
Legal	1	2
Financial	1	2
Educational	1	2

10. How satisfied you are with each of the following services? Please indicate your satisfaction for each service. _20–28_

Services	Definitely Satisfied	Satisfied	Neither Satisfied nor Dissatisfied	Not Satisfied	Definitely Not Satisfied
Daily counseling session	1	2	3	4	5
Legal aid facility	1	2	3	4	5
Library	1	2	3	4	5

11. How much time in a five-minute period does the doctor spend listening (rather than, say, talking) to you? (Please mark one) _29_

    _____ Less than one minute

    _____ About one or two minutes

    _____ More than two minutes

The questionnaire was shown to a reviewer, whose advice was to eliminate Questions 5, 7, and 11, and keep only Question 10. The reviewer stated that surveys are not best for certain types of information. Here's the reasoning:

Question 5 asks for a report of a person's blood pressure. Is it normal? In general, information of this kind can best be obtained from other sources—say, a medical record or directly from a doctor. Many people might have difficulty recalling their blood pressure with precision and also would be at a loss to define "normal" blood pressure.

Question 7 may be all right if you feel confident that the person's recall will be accurate. Otherwise, the records of the center are probably a better source of information about which services are used.

Question 11 asks the patient's to tell how much time the doctor spends listening rather than talking. If you are interested in the patient's perceptions, then the question is fine. If, however, you want data on the actual time the doctor listened rather than talked to the patient, observation by an impartial observer is probably best.

Question 10 is appropriate. Only participants can tell you how satisfied they are. No other source will do as well.

Survey questionnaires are by no means the only source of information for policymakers, evaluators, or researchers, nor are they necessarily the most relevant. Some other sources of information are the following:

- Observations or eyewitness reports; filmed, videotaped, and audiotaped accounts
- Performance tests that require a person to perform a task (such as teaching a lesson to a class); observers assess the effectiveness of the performance
- Written tests of ability or knowledge
- Record reviews that rely on existing documentation, such as reviews of medical and school attendance records; analysis of the content of published and unpublished articles and diaries

Surveys can be used in making policy or planning and evaluating programs and conducting research when the information you need should come directly from people. The data they provide are descriptions of feelings and perceptions, values, habits, and personal background or *demographic* characteristics such as age, health, education, and income.

Sometimes surveys are combined with other sources of information. This is particularly true for evaluations and research.

Example: Surveys Combined With Other Information Sources

- As part of its evaluation of child care programs, the Health Voluntary Agency surveyed parents, children, and staff about their degree of participation and satisfaction. Also, the Agency reviewed financial records to evaluate the costs of each program, and standardized tests were given to appraise how ready children were for school.
- The YMC Corporation is researching how adults learn. Achievement and performance tests are given at regular intervals. In addition, a survey provides supplemental data on how adults like to learn.

QUESTIONNAIRES AND INTERVIEWS: THE HEART OF THE MATTER

All surveys consist of (1) questions and (2) instructions. To get accurate data, you must account for a survey's (3) sampling and design, (4) data processing or "management" and analysis, (5) pilot testing, and (6) response rate. Survey results are given in written and oral reports.

Questions

Information from surveys is obtained by asking questions (sometimes called "items"). The questions may have forced-response choices:

Example: Forced-Choice Item

What is the main advantage of multiple-choice over essay questions?

Can be scored objectively	☐
Are best at measuring complex behaviors	☐
Can have more than one answer	☐
Are the least threatening of the question types	☐

Questions on questionnaires or interview may be open-ended.

Example: Open-Ended Item

What is the main advantage of multiple-choice over essay questions?

Answer here:

_____

_____

_____

_____

The selection, wording, and ordering of questions and answers require careful thought and a reasonable command of language.

Instructions

Surveys always contain instructions for completion. Are all respondents to answer all questions? Is there a time limit? Must all questions be answered? In a survey of viewers' television habits, one section—for example, asking for the programs watched regularly—may be mandatory, whereas a second—calling for demographic or background information on age, educational level, and income—may be optional.

Survey Sample and Design

Surveys are data collection methods used to obtain information from and about people. From and about which people, how often, and when? As soon as you raise questions such as these, you must become concerned with the *sample* and *design* of the survey. The sample is the number and characteristics of people in the survey. The design refers to how often the survey takes place (just once, or *cross-sectional*; over time, or *longitudinal*), whether the participants are selected at random, and how many groups are included.

Consider these three surveys:

- Survey 1: What do graduates from the class of 2005 know about physical fitness?

  Survey method: Mailed, self-administered questionnaire

  Sample: All 1,000 graduates from State College's class of 2005

  How often survey takes place: Just once—at graduation

  How participants are selected: All graduates are eligible

  How many groups: Just one—the class of 2005

  Design: Cross-sectional

- Survey 2: Does knowledge about physical fitness change over a 12-month period among graduates of the class of 2005?

  Survey method: Mailed, self-administered questionnaire

  Sample: All 1,000 graduates from State College's class of 2005

  How often survey takes place: Twice—at graduation and 12 months later

  How participants are selected: All graduates are eligible

  How many groups: Just one—the class of 2005

  Design: Longitudinal

- Survey 3: Over time, do differences exist among graduating classes in their knowledge of physical fitness?

  Survey method: Mailed, self-administered questionnaire

  Sample: A 75% randomly selected sample of graduates from the classes of 2005, 2006, and 2007 to equal a total of 2,250 graduates

  How often survey takes place: Three times—at graduation and 12 and 24 months later

  How participants are selected: Randomly

  How many groups: Three—the classes of 2005, 2006, and 2007

  Design: Longitudinal and comparative

Survey 1 asks for a portrait of the class of 2005's knowledge of physical fitness, and a mailed questionnaire is to be used. This portrait is called a cross-sectional survey design. Survey 2 wants to know about changes in knowledge of physical fitness over a one-year period: from graduation forward 12 months. The design is longitudinal.

Survey 3 is longitudinal because survey data will be collected from each of the three graduating classes over three points in time: at the time of graduation and one and two years later. The design is also comparative because knowledge can be compared between any two and among all three classes at graduation, one year later, two years later, or across all three times. An illustration of the design for Survey 3 can take this form:

	Survey is Given at:	
Class	Time of Graduation	One Year After Graduation
2005		
2006		
2007		

Survey 3 differs from Surveys 1 and 2 in how the graduates are selected for participation. In Survey 3, a 75% sample of graduates will be randomly selected to participate. In the other two surveys, all graduates, not just a sample, are eligible. Random selection means that each graduate has an equal chance of being included.

All three surveys rely on mailed, self-administered questionnaires, but their designs and samples vary.

Planning for Data Analysis

Regardless of your survey's design size, you must think ahead to how you plan to analyze the survey's data.

Will you compute percentages so that your results look like this?

Of the total sample, 50% reported that they were Republicans; 42%, Democrats; 5%, Independent; 1% belonged to the Green Party; and 3% had no party affiliation.

Will you produce averages to appear this way?

The average age of the respondents is 56.4 years. The median educational level is 13 years.

Will you compare groups?

A total of 60% of the men, but only 20% of the women, were Republicans.

Respondents do not differ significantly in satisfaction with the present government.

Will you look for relationships such as this?

The survey found no connection between how liberal or conservative people were and their educational attainments.

High school graduates who were 30 years of age or older were significantly more likely to vote in the last election than were older, less educated respondents.

Will you look for changes over time?

Since 1997, statistically significant differences have been found in the number of men participating in two or more hours of child care per day.

Pilot Testing

A pilot test is a tryout, and its purpose is to help produce a survey form that is usable and that will provide you with the information you need. All types of questionnaires and interviews must be pilot tested. Self-administered questionnaires depend heavily on the clarity of their language, and pilot testing quickly reveals whether people understand the directions you have provided and if they can answer the questions. A pilot test of a face-to-face interview will also tell you about interviewers. Can they follow the form easily? Are the spaces on printed surveys large enough for recording responses? Do interviewers know what to do if the computer "freezes"? Pilot tests can also tell you how much time it takes to complete the survey.

Testing helps make the survey run smoothly. Whenever possible, you should try to duplicate the environment in which the survey is to take place. That might mean obtaining permission from people to be in the tryouts, but not in the survey, even though they are eligible for full participation.

Response Rate

The surveyor wants everyone who is eligible to respond to all questions. Pilot testing helps improve the response rate because it can eliminate severe potential sources of difficulty, such as poorly worded questions and no place to record answers. Furthermore, if the entire set of survey procedures is carefully tested, then this, too, can help the response rate. Before you do a telephone interview, ask: Do you have available a current source of information on people's telephone numbers? Are you willing to make telephone calls at the time the survey respondents are available? Other ways of ensuring good response rates exist, such as keeping surveys short and providing incentives (such as payment for participating).

How high should the response rate be? If you are conducting a large, complex survey, you will want to use statistical procedures to answer this question. If your survey is relatively simple (say, a pool of teachers in a school or nurses in three hospitals), then you have to decide how many people you will need for the results to be believable. If 20 people are eligible for completing a mailed, self-administered questionnaire and only ten respond, you may feel different from the way you will feel if, at another time, 200 of 400 respond. Both surveys have a 50% response rate, but reporting on the views of 10 of 20 people may appear less convincing than telling about 200 of 400. Except when done statistically, the desired response rate tends to be entirely subjective, and the general rule is "higher is better."

Reporting Results

Survey results are reported daily on the Internet, television, and in the newspaper. To many, a survey is a poll, usually of some, but not all, people about an issue of immediate political, social, or economic concern. Survey results typically *look* like this:

Example 1: The Look of Survey Results

Question: If the election were held today, would you vote for Candidate X?

Answer: 125 of 132 (94.6%) men and 200 of 210 (95.2%) women responded. The results are given here in percentages.

	Yes	*No*	*Don't Know*
Men	62	18	20
Women	10	85	5

Example 2: The Look of Survey Results

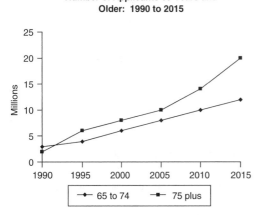

Number of Applicants 65 Years and Older: 1990 to 2015

Source: A Survey of Applicants—Senate Committee

To get results such as these requires many steps, and all surveys follow them:

- Deciding on the type of survey (mailed or online questionnaire, telephone, or face-to-face interviews)
- Selecting the survey's content, writing questions, and trying out the form
- Deciding who should participate (Everyone? A sample of people?) and when (Just once? Each year for five years?)
- Administering the survey (Who should conduct the interview? By when must the questionnaire be returned?)
- Processing the data (Are data to be scanned into the computer? Entered manually? What should be done about missing data?)
- Analyzing and interpreting the results (Did enough people participate? What do the numbers or differences mean? Just how do people feel about Candidate X? Have opinions changed over time?)
- Reporting the results orally or in writing using text, charts, tables, and graphs (Who is the audience? How long should the report be? Which data should be presented?)

No credible survey can omit any single step, although depending on its purposes and resources, some steps will receive more emphasis in any given survey than in another.

SURVEY TYPES: THE FRIENDLY COMPETITION

How do you choose between self-administered questionnaires and interviews? Is a mailed questionnaire better than a telephone interview? How good are Internet-based surveys? Here are some criteria for selecting among the different survey types.

Reliability and Validity

A reliable survey results in consistent information. A valid survey produces accurate information. Reliable and valid surveys are obtained by making sure the definitions and models you use to select questions are grounded in theory or experience. No single survey type starts out with better reliability and validity than another. Choose the survey method that is most precise and accurate for your specific purposes. For example, if you are worried that the people you are surveying cannot read well, an oral interview is likely to produce far better results than a written one. Focus groups and pilot tests help you decide which type to use and if you have done a good job of designing the survey and making it user-friendly. Respondents or survey administrators (the people who do the interviewing or hand out the questionnaires) who have trouble with the survey will use it incorrectly, introducing bias, and that in turn reduces the accuracy of the results. A well-designed, easy-to-use survey always contributes to reliability and validity.

Usefulness or Credibility of Results

The results will be useful if they are valid and if the survey device is one that users accept as the correct one. Find out before you start which method is the one people want. Sometimes the people who will use the results have strong preferences.

Costs

This refers to the financial burden of developing and administering each type of survey. The costs associated with written questionnaires (on-site and mailed) include paper, reproduction, and incentives. Mailed questionnaires require an up-to-date address list (which you may have to purchase), postage, and envelopes. Sometimes you have several follow-up mailings, adding to the costs.

The costs of face-to-face and telephone interviews include purchasing a telephone system and paying for miscalled and out-of-date telephone numbers as well as hang ups. You also need to pay for writing a script for the interviewer, training the interviewers, monitoring the quality of the interviews, and providing incentives to respondents.

Computer-based and online surveys require extensive development and testing. Any mistakes in programming or analysis can invalidate the survey's findings. Costs mount if you need to purchase consultants and computers. Online surveys require special programming expertise, a connection to the Internet, and special methods of ensuring privacy and confidentiality. Also, for some time to come, certain respondents (such as some who have not grown up with computers, do not have access to the Internet, or prefer to take cyberspace slowly) will continue to mistrust online surveys. It is always wise to offer at least two modes of survey administration—say, online or mail. Be prepared to compare groups of respondents who choose differing survey types to make certain that they are alike in important ways. Are they the same age? Gender? If you find differences, you may have to regard each set of respondents as a separate sample.

Table 1.1 compares the advantages and disadvantages of the major survey types and reminds you of their special needs and costs.

A SURVEY CONTINUUM: FROM SPECIFIC TO GENERAL USE

Surveys have become a major means of collecting data to answer questions about health and social, economic, and political life. How extensive and scientific must a survey be?

Compare these two surveys:

Example: Survey With a Specific Use

The directors of the Neighborhood Halfway Houses want to provide services that are appropriate for residents. At present, many complaints have arisen over the lack of adequate fitness facilities. A survey will be conducted to poll the five health care providers, 100 residents, and ten full- and part-time staff to find out what facilities are desirable and affordable.

Example: Survey With a General Use

The County Health Department is concerned with the effectiveness of its 10 halfway houses. Together, the 10 houses have 20,000 residents and 220 full- and part-time staff. This County has negotiated arrangements for health care services from a number of providers in the public and private sectors. As part of its effectiveness study, This County is surveying a random sample of residents, staff, and providers at all houses. NextDoor County is interested in adopting This County's halfway house model and is anxiously waiting for the results of the survey and the evaluation.

Table 1.1   Comparing Survey Types

	Self-Administered			Interviews	
	Mailed	*On-Site*	*Online*	*Telephone*	*In-Person*
Characteristics	Paper and pencil	Paper and pencil	Internet based	Can be done with written script or computer assisted	Can be done with a written script or computer assisted
Advantages	Can reach large geographic areas People are used to completing paper-and-pencil surveys Can take the survey with you and complete it anywhere	Information is obtained immediately Questions about survey can be asked by respondents as they arise In some cases, surveys can be done with groups of people	Worldwide Order of questions can be preprogrammed Only "legal" answers are accepted Can give respondent links that explain unfamiliar words and help with difficult questions Data are automatically entered and can be automatically analyzed	Can explore answers with respondents Can assist respondent with unfamiliar words	Same as telephone
Disadvantages	Need a motivated sample to return survey. Many people think they have too much to do without also having to complete surveys Respondents must be able to read, see, and write	Limited to responses from just those who are on site Respondents must be able to read, see, and write	Need reliable access to Internet Respondent must be able to use a browser Browser must support survey graphics System can go down or be unreliable	Need trained interviewers Need to make sure respondent is home If using computer-assisted interviews, will need technical expertise to program them	Need trained interviewers Must find a suitable place to conduct interview
Special needs	Up-to-date address list Follow-up mailings Incentives	Space and privacy for respondent to complete the survey	Technical expertise Convincing method of ensuring privacy and confidentiality	Up-to-date phone numbers Schedule for reaching respondents May need a sampling expert for random digit dialing Incentives	If on-site, need space and privacy May be difficult or dangerous to go to person's home
Costs	Printing, paper, envelopes, stamps, incentives	Printing, paper, incentives, survey supervisor, and possibly space for respondent to work	Mainly technical (e.g., someone who is experienced in designing online surveys)	Training, incentives, telephones and telephone charges, computers and technical expertise, sampling expert, incentives	Training, space, travel, incentives

The justification for the first survey is one halfway house's concern with its own needs. The reason for the second is This County's interest in the effectiveness of all its halfway houses. Also, NextDoor County is interested in the survey's results. Survey 1, with its limited impact, can be relatively informal in its methods. Survey 2, on the other hand, must be rigorous in its sampling plan, questionnaire construction, and data analysis and interpretation. Survey 1 is concerned primarily with usefulness.

Survey 2 is also concerned with validity and generalizability: If adapted in another place (NextDoor County), will This County's halfway house model be equally effective?

Each time you do a survey, you must evaluate where its purposes fall on a continuum that goes from specific to general use. You have some leeway with a survey designed to meet very specific needs. All surveys that aim to be generalizable in their findings must be conducted with rigor.

2

THE SURVEY FORM

Questions, Scales, and Appearance

OVERVIEW

To decide on a survey's content, you have to define the attitude, belief, value, or idea being measured. For example, what is meant by fear? By a liberal perspective? By self-efficacy? Also ask: Which questions must be asked in a valid survey if I want to measure fear [or a liberal perspective or self-efficacy]? Can I get the information I need from a survey, or is some other data collection method a better way to go?

Survey questions may be closed or open-ended. Closed questions with several choices are easier to score than are open-ended, short answer, essay questions. Open-ended questions give respondents an opportunity to state a position in their own words; unfortunately, these words may be difficult to interpret.

When writing questions, use standard English; keep questions concrete and close to the respondents' experience; become aware of words, names, and views that might automatically bias your results; check your own biases; do not get too personal; and use a single thought in each question.

The responses to closed questions can take the form of yes–no answers, checklists, and rating scales. Rating scales may be graphic, but often they ask respondents to make comparisons in the form of ranks (1 = *top*, 10 = *bottom*) or use gradations (1 = *definitely agree*, 2 = *agree*, 3 = *disagree*, 4 = *definitely disagree*) and continuums (someone's age). The numerical values assigned to rating scales can be classified as categorical, ordinal, and continuous. Each has characteristics that must be considered when you analyze the results of your survey.

Surveyors are often interested in responses to individual items such as the number of people who will vote for Candidate X or how often women between 65 and 80 years of age visit a doctor in a three-month period. Sometimes they are concerned with a score on a group of items that collectively represent respondents' views, health status, or feelings.

The Content Is the Message

Once you have decided that a survey is the method you want to use to gather data, you must consider the content or topics it will include.

Suppose you are evaluating a youth center's progress and that your main task is to find out whether the program's objectives have been achieved. Say that one of the objectives is to raise young people's self-esteem by providing them with education, jobs, financial help, and medical and mental health assistance. Suppose also that you decide to survey the young program participants to find out about their self-esteem. How would you determine which content to include?

To select the content of a survey you have to define your terms and clarify what you need and can get from asking people about their views.

Define the Terms

Many human attitudes and feelings, such as self-esteem, are subject to a range of definitions. Does self-esteem mean feeling good about oneself, and if so, what does feeling good mean? The surveyor can answer questions such as this by reviewing the research (in this case, the literature on self-esteem) to find out what is known and theorized about a concept such as self-esteem, consulting with experts, or defining the concept for himself or herself. The problem with using your own definition is that others may not be convinced of its validity. When using a theoretical concept such as self-esteem, it is probably best to adopt a respected point of view, and even, if possible, an already existing and tested survey form.

Of course, for many surveys you will not be measuring theoretical ideas, but even so, you must define your terms. Suppose you are assessing a community's needs for health services. The terms *needs* and *health services* would certainly require definition because you can define them with respect to the type and nature of services required (outpatient clinics? hospitals? home visits?) and how convenient (time of day when doctors should be available) or how continuous they should be (must the same doctor always be available?).

Select Your Information Needs or Hypotheses

Suppose two surveyors choose the same definition of self-esteem for their evaluation study of the youth center. Depending on the circumstances, Surveyor 1 might decide to focus on self-esteem in relation to feelings of general well-being, whereas Surveyor 2 may be concerned with feelings of self-esteem only as they manifest themselves in school or at work. Certainly Surveyors 1 and 2, with their different orientations, will be asking different questions. The results will yield different kinds of information. Surveyor 1, with a concern for general self-esteem, may not even cover work or school and will not be able to provide data on these topics. Surveyor 2, with his or her special interests in school and work, probably will not provide information on participant self-esteem with respect to personal relationships. The messages revealed by each survey will clearly be different.

Say you are interested in whether participants in the youth center had their general self-esteem enhanced after two years' participation in the program and that you have defined your terms to conform to an accepted theory of adolescent personality. To make sure you get all the data you need, you must ask the question, What information do I want and must therefore make certain I will be collecting? Remember, if you do not ask for it, you cannot report it later!

Here are some typical questions that the evaluator of the youth center could ask:

1. Is there a relationship between general feelings of self-esteem and whether the participant is a boy or girl?

2. Do participants' self-esteem differ depending on how long they have been in the program?

These two questions suggest that the survey must get data on three topics:

- General feelings of self-esteem
- Gender of participant
- Length of participation in the program

If any of these topics is omitted, the surveyor of the youth center cannot answer the two evaluation questions. After all, in this case the survey is being done only for the evaluation.

Make Sure You Can Get the Information Needed

In some cases, people may be reluctant to reveal their opinions. The evaluator of the youth center, for example, may discover that many young people are reluctant to answer questions about their feelings. In other cases, potential survey respondents may simply be unable to provide answers. Suppose you want to ask participants who have been attending the youth center for about six months about their attitudes toward school just before entering the center's program. Many may have forgotten. Inability to answer questions is not unique and is a major problem with accurately predicting voters' preferences in national elections. It often takes time for people to settle on a candidate, and some people change their opinions several times over the course of a campaign. That is one reason polls produce results that differ among themselves and from one point in time to another.

If you are not certain you can get the information you need from a survey, remove the topic and find another data source, such as observations or reviews of records such as diaries and reports of school attendance or hospital admissions.

Do Not Ask for Information Unless You Can Act on It

In a survey of a community's needs for health services, it would be unfair to have people rate their preference for a trauma center if the community is unable to support such a service. Remember that the content of a survey can affect respondent's views and expectations. Why raise hopes that you cannot or will not fulfill?

Once you have selected the content and set the survey's boundaries, your next task is to actually write the questions. Write more questions than you plan to use because several will probably be rejected as unsuitable. First drafts often have questions for which everyone gives the same answer or no one gives any answer at all. Before deciding on the number and sequence of questions, you must be sure that you cover the complete domain of content you have identified as important to the survey. You may want to keep a list such as the following one used by the surveyor of participant satisfaction with the youth center. As you can see, this survey will not cover staff sensitivity but will focus instead on consideration, accessibility, and availability of services.

Example: Plan for Survey of Satisfaction With the Youth Center

Topics	Number of Questions
1. Staff sensitivity	
Counselor usually listens	0
Counselor is available when needed	0
Appointment staff courteous	0
.	
.	
.	
.	
2. Accessibility of services	
Hours are convenient	卌
Public transportation	卌 I
3. Consideration of participant's needs	
Translation assistance	卌
Ease of getting appointments	卌 I
Waiting times	卌 I
.	
.	
.	
.	
10. Availability of needed services	
Medical	卌 卌
Educational	卌 卌 I

Writing Questions

Open-Ended and Closed Questions

Survey items may take the form of questions:

Example: Open-Ended Question

1. How courteous are the people who make your appointments?

_____

_____

_____

Or they may be worded as statements:

Example: Closed Question

Circle your agreement or disagreement with the following:

2. The people who make my appointments are courteous.

	Circle one
Definitely agree	1
Agree	2
Disagree	3
Definitely disagree	4

Sometimes survey items are open-ended, meaning that the respondents agree to answer the question or respond to the statement in their own words. Question 1 is open-ended. At other times, survey items force the respondent to choose from preselected alternatives as in Question 2.

The overwhelming majority of surveys rely on multiple-choice questions because they have proven themselves to be the more efficient and ultimately more reliable. Their efficiency comes from being easy to use, score, and enter data. Also, their reliability is enhanced because of the uniform data they provide; everyone responds in terms of the same options (agree or disagree, frequently or infrequently, and so on).

Open-ended questions can offer insight into why people believe the things they do, but interpreting them can be extremely difficult unless they are accompanied by an elaborate coding system and people are trained to classify the data they get within the system.

Consider these two answers to a question from a survey of participants in an elementary school teaching program.

Example: Open-Ended Question for Elementary School Teaching Program

Question: What were the three most useful parts of the program?

_____

_____

_____

Answers: _Respondent A_

Instructor's lectures

The field experience

Textbook

Respondent B

Instructor

Teaching in the classroom

The most useful part was the excellent atmosphere for learning provided by the program.

It is not easy to compare A's and B's responses. Respondent B lists the instructor as useful. Does this mean that the instructor is a useful resource in general, and how does this compare with Respondent A's view that the instructor's lectures were useful? In other words, are A and B giving the same answer? Respondent A says the textbook was useful. If only one text was used in the program, then A and B gave the same answer. But because the two recorded responses are different, some guessing or interpretation of what is meant is necessary.

Respondent A and B each mentioned something that the other did not: field experience and learning atmosphere. If these were equally important, then they could be analyzed individually. But suppose neither was particularly significant from the perspective of the survey's users. Would they then be assigned to a category labeled something like "miscellaneous"? Categories called miscellaneous usually are assigned all the difficult responses, and before you know it, miscellaneous can become the largest category of all.

Although it may be relatively easy for a respondent to answer an open-ended question, analysis and interpretation are quite complicated. The following closed question could have been used to obtain the same information with the added result of making the responses easy to interpret.

Example: Closed Question for Elementary School Teaching Program

	Circle One Choice			
	Definitely Not Satisfied	Not Satisfied	Satisfied	Definitely Satisfied
a. The textbook, *Teaching in the Classroom*	4	3	2	1
b. The instructor's knowledge of subject matter	4	3	2	1
c. The practicality of lecture topics	4	3	2	1
d. The field experience	4	3	2	1
e. Other, specify	4	3	2	1

ORGANIZING RESPONSES TO OPEN-ENDED SURVEY ITEMS: DO YOU GET ANY SATISFACTION?

A very common use of a survey is to find out whether people are satisfied with a new product, service, or program. Their opinions provide important insights into why new ideas or ways of doing things do or do not get used.

One open-ended set of questions that is particularly appropriate for getting at satisfaction requires collecting information about what people like best (LB) about the product or service and what they like least (LL).

Here is how the LB/LL technique works:

Step 1

Ask respondents to list what is good and what is bad. Always set a limit on the number of responses: "List at least one thing, but no more than three things, you liked best about the conference." If participants cannot come up with three responses, they can leave blank spaces or write "none." If they give more than three, you can keep or discard the extras, depending on the information you need.

Instead of asking about the conference as a whole, you may want to focus on some particular aspect: "List at least one thing, but no more than three things, you liked best about the workshops."

Step 2: Coding LB/LL Data

Once you have all the responses, the next step is to categorize and code them. To do this, you can create categories based on your review of the responses, or you can create categories based on past experience with similar programs.

Try to keep the categories as precise as possible—that is, more categories rather than fewer—because it is easier to combine them later if necessary than it is to break them up.

Suppose these are typical answers participants gave to the question on what they liked least about the conference:

- Some people did all the talking.
- The instructor didn't always listen.
- I couldn't say anything without being interrupted.
- Too much noise and confusion.
- Some participants were ignored.
- The instructor didn't take control.
- I didn't get a chance to say anything.
- Smith and Jones were the only ones who talked.
- The instructor didn't seem to care.
- I couldn't hear myself think.

You might categorize and code these as follows:

Example LB/LL: Response Categories

	Code
Instructor didn't listen (ignored participants; didn't seem to care)	1
Some people monopolized discussion (did all the talking; couldn't say anything; Smith and Jones were the only ones who talked)	2
Disorderly environment (too much noise; instructor didn't take control; couldn't hear myself think)	3

Now match your codes and the responses:

Example LB/LL: Participant Responses

	Code
Participant A	
Instructor didn't always listen	1
I couldn't hear myself think	3
I couldn't say anything without being interrupted	2
Participant B	
Instructor didn't always listen	1
The instructor didn't take control when things got noisy	3
The instructor ignored some students	3
Participant C	
I didn't get a chance to say anything	2

To make sure you assigned the codes correctly, you may want to establish their reliability. Are they clear enough so that at least two raters would assign the same code for a given response?

Step 3: LB/LL Data

When you are satisfied about reliability, the next step is to count the number of responses for each code.

Here's how to do this for ten participants:

Example LB/LL: Number of Responses for Each Code

	Codes			
Participant	1	2	3	Total
A	1	1	1	3
B	1		2	3
C		2	1	3
D		1	2	3
E		3		3
F		2	1	3
G		2	1	3
H		2	1	3
I		3	2	5
J		1		1
	2	17	11	30

Look at the number of responses in each category. The ten participants listed a total of 30 things they liked least about the small group discussion. Seventeen of 30 (more than 50%) were assigned to the same category, Code 2, and the surveyor could justly argue that, based on the data, what the participants tended to like least about the workshops was that some people monopolized the discussions and others did not get a chance to say anything.

Next count the *number of* participants whose answers were assigned to each code. For example, only participants A and B gave answers that were coded 1.

Example LB/LL: Participants' Response Pattern

Code	No. of Participants Listing a Response Assigned to This Code	Which Participants?
1	2	A, B
2	9	All but B
3	8	All but E and J

Look at the number of participants whose responses fit each category. Because eight or nine of the ten participants gave responses that fell into the same two categories (Codes 2 and 3), their opinions probably represent those of the entire group. It is safe to add that participants also disliked the disorderly atmosphere that prevailed during the workshops. They complained that the noise made it hard to think clearly, and the instructor did not take control.

When respondents agree with one another, there will be only a few types of answers, and these will be listed by many people. If respondents disagree, many different kinds of answers will turn up on their lists, and only a few people (fewer than 10%) will be associated with each type.

Interpreting LB/LL data gets more complex when you have many participants and responses to categorize. Suppose, for example, you ask 100 participants to indicate which aspects of a health education program they liked best.

First you must decide on your response categories and assign each one a code. Then try this:

1. Put the codes in rank order. That is, if the largest number of participants chose responses that are assigned to Code 3, list Code 3 first.

2. Calculate the percentage of students assigned to each code. If 40 of 100 students made responses that were assigned a code of 3, then the calculation would be 40%.

3. Count the number of responses assigned to each code.

4. Calculate the percentage of responses assigned to each code. If 117 responses from a total of 400 were assigned to Code 3, then 29.25% or 117/400 of responses were for Code 3.

5. Calculate the cumulative percentage of responses by adding the percentages together: 29.25% plus 20.25% = 49.50%.

6. Below is a table that summarizes these steps with some hypothetical data.

Example LB/LL: Summary of Responses

Response Categories (With Codes in Rank Order)	Percentage of Participants Assigned to Each Code (100 Participants)	Number of Responses Assigned to Each Code (100 Participants)	Percentage of Responses Assigned to Each Code	Cumulative Percentage of Responses Assigned to Each Code
3	40	117	29.25	29.25
4	34	81	20.25	49.50
7	32	78	19.50	69.00
8	20	35	8.75	77.25
10	17	30	7.50	85.25
1	15	29	7.25	92.50
6	10	14	3.50	96.00
2	5	10	2.50	98.50
9	3	5	1.25	99.75
5	1	1	0.25	100.00

	3	4	7	8	10	1	6	2	9	5
% Responses per code	40	34	32	20	17	15	10	5	3	1
Cumulative % Responses per code	29.25	49.5	69	77.25	85.25	92.5	96	98.5	99.75	100

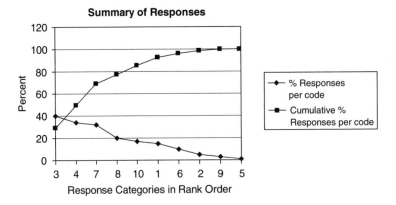

As you can see, the response categories are rank ordered along the X-axis according to the number of participants assigned to each code. The Y-axis represents percentages.

For each response category, you should look for two points on the X-axis: the percentage of participants and the cumulative percentage of responses. First, the cumulative percentages of responses are joined with a square (■). Next, some of the points representing percentages of participants are joined with a diamond (♦).

The graph shows that responses coded as 3, 4, and 7 seem to cluster together. They are the categories to be emphasized because the highest percentages of participants were assigned to these codes, and they account for a total of 69% of all responses.

Items 8, 10, and 1 form a second intuitive cluster that represents 23.5% of all responses. Taken together, responses coded as 3, 4, 7, 8, 10, and 1 account for 92.5% of the total.

RULES FOR WRITING CLOSED SURVEY QUESTIONS

Multiple choice, closed-ended survey questions consist of a stem, which presents a problem (typically in the form of a statement, a question, a brief case history, or situation) followed by several alternative choices or solutions. Here are rules for their construction.

1. *Each Question Should Be Meaningful to Respondents.* In a survey of political views, the questions should be about the political process, parties, candidates, and so on. If you introduce other questions that have no readily obvious purpose, such as those about age or gender, you might want to explain why they are being asked: "We are asking some personal questions so that we can look for connections between people's backgrounds and their views . . ."

2. *Use Standard English.* Because you want an accurate answer to each survey item, you must use conventional grammar, spelling, and syntax. Avoid specialized words (unless you are testing people's knowledge of them) and abbreviations, and make sure that your items are not so lengthy that you are actually testing reading or vocabulary.

Example: Item-Writing Skills—Length, Clarity, Abbreviations, and Jargon

Length

Poor: The paucity of psychometric scales with high degrees of stability and construct validity is most bothersome to surveyors when measuring people's:

1. Economic characteristics
2. Feelings
3. Knowledge
4. Health

Better: The lack of reliable and valid methods causes surveyors the most problems when measuring people's:

1. Economic characteristics
2. Feelings
3. Knowledge
4. Health

Clarity

Poor: What remedy do you usually use for stomach-aches?

Better: Which brand of medicine do you usually use for stomachaches?

Abbreviations

Poor: Which political party is responsible for the expanding size of the GDP?
1. Republican
2. Democrat

Better: Which political party is responsible for the diminishing size of the gross domestic product?
1. Republican
2. Democrat

Jargon

Poor: In your view, which dyad is most responsible for feelings of trust in early childhood?
1. Mother and father
2. Father and sibling
3. Mother and sibling

Better: In your view, which family combination is most responsible for feelings of trust in early childhood?
1. Mother and father
2. Father and brother or sister
3. Mother and brother or sister

---

3. *Make Questions Concrete.* Questions should be close to the respondent's personal experience.

Example: Item-Writing Skills—Concrete Questions

Less concrete:	Do you think other people would enjoy the book?
More concrete:	Have you recommended the book to anyone else?

Asking respondents if they think others would enjoy a book is more abstract than asking if they recommended it to others. Who are the "others"? Can you be sure the respondent knows about other people's enjoyment with respect to the book? The farther you remove a question from the respondent's direct experience, the closer you come to the problems associated with remembering.

Consider this:

Example: Item-Writing Skills—Specificity of Questions

Five companies in a small city were surveyed to find out about their attitudes toward hiring women for managerial positions. One survey question asked, "Do you think women have as good a chance as men for managerial positions?" A friend of the surveyor pointed out that a better way of asking the question was, "At (fill in name of company), do women have as good a chance as men for managerial positions?"

Be careful not to err on the concrete side. If you ask people how many hours of television they watched each day for the past week, you should be sure that no reason exists for believing that the past week was unusual so that the data would not be representative of a "true" week's worth of TV viewing. Among the factors that might affect viewers' habits are television specials such as the Olympics and cataclysms such as plane crashes, earthquakes, floods, and fires.

4. *Avoid Biased Words and Phrases.* Certain names, places, and views are emotionally charged. When included in a survey, they unfairly influence people's responses. Words such as *president, abortion, terrorist,* and *alcoholic* are examples.

Suppose you are surveying people who had just been through a diet program. Which words should you use: *thin* or *slender*; *portly, heavy,* or *fat*?

Remember this?

I am firm.

You are stubborn.

He is a pig-headed fool.

Look at these questions.

Would you vote for Roger Fields?

Would you vote for Dr. Roger Fields?

Would you vote for Roger Fields, a liberal?

Although Roger Fields appears to be the most neutral description of the candidate, it may be considered the least informative. Yet the introduction of Dr. or liberal may bias the responses.

5. *Check Your Own Biases.* An additional source of bias is present when survey writers are unaware of their own position toward a topic. Look at this:

Example: Item-Writing Skills—Hidden Biases

Poor: Do you think the liberals and conservatives will soon reach a greater degree of understanding?

Poor: Do you think the liberals and conservatives will continue their present poor level of understanding?

When you are asking questions that you suspect encourage strong views on either side, it is helpful to have them reviewed. Ask your reviewer if the wording is unbiased and acceptable to persons holding contrary opinions. For a survey of people's views on the relationship between the liberals and the conservatives, you might ask:

Example: Item-Writing Skills—Hidden Biases

Better: In your opinion, in the next four years, how is the relationship between the liberals and the conservatives likely to change?

Much improvement
Some improvement
Some worsening
Much worsening
Impossible to predict

6. *Use Caution When Asking for Personal Information.* Another source of bias may result from questions that may intimidate the respondent. Questions such as, "How much do you earn each year?" "Are you single or divorced?" "How do you feel about your teacher, counselor, or doctor?" are personal and may offend some people who might then refuse to give the true answers. When personal information is essential to the survey, you can ask questions in the least emotionally charged way if you provide categories of responses.

Example: Question-Writing Skills—Very Personal Questions

Poor: What was your annual income last year?

$_____

Better: In which category does your annual income last year fit best?

Below $10,000
Between $10,001 and $20,000
Between $20,001 and $40,000
Between $40,001 and $75,000
Over $75,001

Categories of responses are generally preferred for very sensitive questions because they do not specifically identify the respondent and appear less personal.

7. *Each Question Should Have Just One Thought.* Do not use questions in which a respondent's truthful answer could be both yes and no at the same time or agree and disagree at the same time.

Example: Question-Writing Skills—One Thought per Question

Poor: Should the United States cut its military or domestic spending?

Yes
No
Don't know

Better: Should the United States substantially reduce its military spending?

Yes
No
Don't know

or

Should the United States allocate more money to domestic programs?

Yes
No
Don't know

or

If the United States reduced its military spending, should it use the funds for domestic programs?

    Yes

    No

    Don't know

RESPONSES FOR CLOSED QUESTIONS

Yes and No

The responses in a survey with closed questions can take several forms.

Example: Yes and No Responses

Have you graduated from college?

    Yes

    No

Does your car have four-wheel drive?

    Yes

    No

    Don't know

Yes and no responses are simple to use and score. But a slight misinterpretation means that the answer will be exactly opposite from what the respondent really means. Also, in some cases, asking for absolutely negative or positive views may result in the participant's refusal to answer or choice of a "don't know."

Checklist

A checklist provides respondents with a series of answers. They may choose just one or more answers depending on the instructions.

Example: Checklist Responses in Which Respondent Must Choose One From a List of Several

(One answer only)

Which of the following medicines do you prefer most for treating a headache?

	Circle One
I don't take medicine for headaches	1
Aspirin	2
Tylenol	3
Advil	4
Excedrin	5
Other, specify _____	6

Example: Checklist Responses That Respondents Answer Yes, No, or Don't Know for Each Item in a List

	Check (☑) One Box On Each Line		
In the past 12 months, has a doctor or other health care worker told you that you have any of the following:	*No*	*Yes*	*Don't Know*
a. Hepatitis	☐	☐	☐
b. Gastritis	☐	☐	☐
c. Ulcer of the stomach or small intestine	☐	☐	☐
d. Pancreatitis	☐	☐	☐
e. Depression, anxiety, or another emotional or mental problem	☐	☐	☐

Checklists help remind respondents of some things they might have forgotten. If you simply asked people to list their medications, chances are some would forget what they have taken. Also, checklists provide the spelling for difficult words. A problem with them is that respondents might think a choice is familiar when it is not. Did they take penicillin or ampicillin? Was it this month or last? Also, it is somewhat difficult to format and interpret responses to checklists where multiple answers can be given. Suppose in the second example that a person checks aspirin and codeine but fails to indicate whether or not the other medicines were taken. Can you assume that the others were not taken, or is it possible that they were, but the person did not bother to complete the item?

Online Survey Questions

Web surveys look and often act like self-administered questionnaires. Look at the example below:

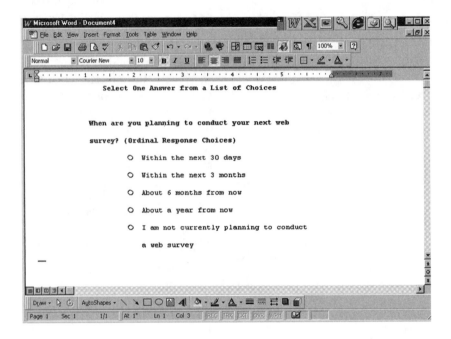

The rules for writing questions for the Web are almost exactly the same as for other self-administered paper-and-pencil and computer-based surveys. They are different, however, in that they can easily incorporate color and graphics to make them attractive. With sufficient resources, they may also be created to provide respondents with access to sophisticated audio and visual aids. Such aids may assist respondents in understanding terms they cannot read. Even though the technology is available to supplement Web surveys with audio and visual aids, respondents may not have the equipment (e.g., a sound card) that will enable them to take advantage of these features.

But even if respondents have access to the technology, they may not know how to use it appropriately, if at all. If you are planning to conduct a Web survey, you must be concerned with the respondent's "computer literacy." Although definitions of computer literacy vary, it usually means having the skills to use the keyboard, mouse, or both to scroll through the screen and questionnaire, enter the answers, and perform the operations necessary to go to the next question and submit the completed questionnaire. In some cases, respondents will have to click on an e-mail attachment to get to the survey or enter an address (URL), login ID, and password to find it.

Computer literacy varies greatly. Some people can use practically all types of software, whereas others are mainly familiar with sending e-mail and shopping on the Internet.

A major and important difference between Web questions and other question types is that even in small surveys (say, those on your company's Intranet), you can easily use color and simple graphics to make the survey attractive. Remember if you plan to use graphics, make sure that respondents can easily download the survey. Do they have compatible software? Do they have enough space to store the file? In fact, an important and currently unanswered question about online surveys is whether they are a technological advance in self-administered survey design or if they are actually a different type of survey altogether.

The drop-down list is unique to online surveys. It is often used to save space when a long list of responses is possible. For instance, if you want to know the country in which the respondent lives, you can save a great deal of screen space by providing a drop-down list of countries rather than printing the list itself.

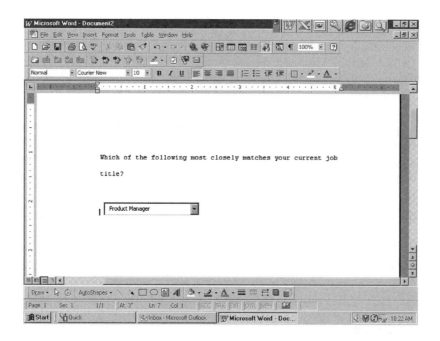

RATING SCALES

With rating scales, the respondent places the item being rated at some point along a continuum or in any one of an ordered series of categories. A numerical value is assigned to the point or category. There are four types of rating or measurement scales.

1. *Categorical.* These are sometimes called nominal responses scales and refer to answers given by people about the groups to which they belong: gender, religious affiliation, school, or college last attended.

Example: Categorical Rating Scale

What is the newborn's gender?

	Circle One
Male	1
Female	2

2. *Ordinal.* These scales require that respondents place answers in rank order. A person's economic status (high, medium, or low) would provide an ordinal measurement. A measure of whether an individual strongly agreed with a statement, agreed, disagreed, or strongly disagreed is considered an ordinal measure by some people and as an interval measure by others.

Example: Ordinal Rating Scale

What is the highest level of education that you achieved?

	Circle One
Elementary school	1
Some high school	2
High school graduate	3
Some college	4
College graduate	5
Postgraduate	6

3. *Continuous Scales*

Type 1: Interval. With these measurement scales, the distances between numbers have a real meaning. Annual income, for example, may be placed in intervals. The $10,000 difference between $20,000 and $30,000 a year means the same as the difference between $50,000 and $60,000 a year. However, having an income of $20,000 does not automatically mean that you are twice as rich as the person whose income is $10,000. Too many variables intervene, such as the number of people in the family, eligibility for assistance, savings, home ownership, and so on.

Example: Interval Rating Scale

How many millions of dollars would you be willing to spend on a three-bedroom, two-bathroom house on one-half acre with a pool in Beverly Hills estates?

1. $1,000,000 to $1,500,000

2. $1,500,001 to $2,000,000

3. $2,000,001 to $2,500,000

4. Money is no object

Type 2: Ratio. Height and weight are ratio scales. If you weigh 120 pounds and I weigh 240 pounds, I am twice as heavy as you. A ratio scale, like an interval scale, is one in which adjoining units on the scale are always equidistant from each other, no matter where they are on the scale. In addition, the ratio scale has a true zero. A ruler represents a ratio scale: The inch difference between seven inches and eight inches is the same as the difference between nine inches and ten inches, and zero means the absence of length. With the ratio scale, you can say that six inches is twice as long as three inches.

Example: Ratio Scale

How many pounds did you weigh on your last check up?

Weight in pounds: ☐ ☐ ☐

The distinctions between categorical, ordinal, and continuous scales are important because they determine the kinds of statistical treatments you can use. For example, the appropriate measure of an average score for use with a categorical scale is the mode, whereas the median may be used with an ordinal scale and the mean with a continuous scale (see Chapter 6).

Graphic Scales

For a survey opinion on the city council's effectiveness in resolving certain issues, a graphic scale could resemble that shown in the following example.

Example: Graphic Rating Scale for Assessing a City Council's Effectiveness

Directions:

Make an X on the line that shows your opinion about the city council's effectiveness in resolving the following three issues:

	Very Effective	In Between	Very Ineffective	
Cleaning the environment	1	3	5	7	9
New public transportation	1	3	5	7	9
Hiring new teachers	1	3	5	7	9

Graphic scales are a kind of rating scale in which the continuum of responses is visual. Because of this, you do not have to name all the points on the scale. In this example, only three points are identified: very effective, neutral, very ineffective.

Graphic scales are relatively easy to use. Be careful to put the description as close as possible to the points they represent. If you use the same scale twice for different parts of the questionnaire, be sure they have the same distances between points.

Example: Poor Formatting of Graphic Scales

If you use this scale, stay with it.

Very Effective				Very Ineffective
1	3	5	7	9

Do not also use this scale in the same survey or question.

A major disadvantage of graphic scales is that they are sometimes hard to interpret. Look how these three respondents marked the same graphic scale:

Example: Interpreting Graphic Scales

	Agree	Neutral	Disagree
Respondent A		X	
	1	2	3
Respondent B	X		
	1	2	3
Respondent C		X	
	1	2	3

Respondent A has clearly selected a neutral rating. But what about Respondents B and C? Both appear somewhat neutral, with B agreeing more than A and C, and C disagreeing more than either. You can decide to assign all ratings to the nearest point—in this case, 2—or you can assume a true continuum and assign Respondent B a rating of 1.75 and Respondent C a rating of 2.20. Because all graphic scales share this problem in interpretation, the surveyor will always have to decide on a strategy for making sense of the respondents' ratings.

Comparative Rating Scales

Comparative rating scales rely on relative judgments. The most common is the rank order, which is a type of ordinal scale.

Example: Rank Order Scale

Please rank the following five individuals according to their writing ability. The top ranked should be assigned the number 1 and the lowest ranked the number 5.

_____ Fay Gross

_____ Betty Bass

_____ Edward Romney

_____ Alexander Rulman

_____ Marvin Jackson

Another type of comparative scale enables you to contrast a single specific object in terms of a general situation.

Example: Comparative Rating Scale

Please compare the Imperial Thai Restaurant to others in Los Angeles.

Check one

☐ It is better than most.

☐ It is about the same as most.

☐ It is not as good as most.

To ensure that comparative rating scales provide accurate information, you have to be certain that the respondents are in a position to make comparisons. Do they have experience in judging writing skills? Are they fully acquainted with restaurants in Los Angeles?

Category Scales or Gradations

When raters use category scales, they select one of a limited number of categories that are previously ordered with respect to their position on some scale:

Example: Category Scales

Frequently

Sometimes

Almost never

Very favorable

Favorable

Neither favorable nor unfavorable

Unfavorable

Very unfavorable

Strongly approve

Approve

Neither approve nor disapprove

Disapprove

Strongly disapprove

Definitely agree

Probably agree

Neither agree nor disagree

Probably don't agree

Definitely don't agree

Are category scales ordinal or continuous? Technically, they are ordinal, but in practice, they are regarded and analyzed as if they were continuous. In any case, they are easy to use and interpret. How many categories should there be? Some people use as many as nine categories and others as few as two (yes, no). An even number of choices—say, four—forces the respondent away from the middle ground ("neither agree nor disagree.") But the needs of the survey and skills of the respondent must determine the number of categories. If very precise information is needed, the respondents are willing and able to give it, and you have the resources to collect it, use many categories (between 7 and 9); otherwise, use fewer.

Consider these two situations:

Example: Selecting the Number of Categories

1. A four-minute telephone interview was conducted to find out how often families with working mothers ate dinner in restaurants. The question was asked: "In a typical month, how often does your family eat dinner in a restaurant?" The response choices were "two or more times a week," "once a week," or "less than once a week."

2. Physicians were asked to rate the appropriateness of a comprehensive list of reasons for performing selected surgical procedures such as coronary artery bypass graft surgery and gallbladder removal. An appropriate reason was defined as one for which benefits to patients outweighed risks. A scale of 1 to 9 was used: 1 = *definitely inappropriate*, whereas 9 = *definitely appropriate*.

In Situation 1, the four-minute interview dictated short responses. In Situation 2, physicians were asked to use their expertise to give fairly refined ratings.

SCALING

Additive Scales

Most surveys are designed so that each individual item counts. In a survey of people's attitudes toward living in a trailer park, you might ask 12 questions, each of which is designed in itself to be used to analyze attitudes and therefore is scored separately. Suppose you collected information like this:

- Length of time living in this trailer park
- Ever lived in one before
- Satisfaction with trailer's accommodations
- Satisfaction with park's accommodations
- Satisfaction with quality of lifestyle
- Amenities in trailer
- Age of trailer
- Age of car
- Type of car
- Age of respondent
- Gender of respondent
- Annual income

With this information, you could report on each fact individually or you could look for relationships:

- Between age of respondent and satisfaction with quality of lifestyle
- Between gender and length of time living in the trailer park

Other surveys are different, however, in that the items do not count individually; they must be combined to get a score.

Consider this:

Example: A Survey With an Additive Scale

Doctors at University Medical Center observed that many of their very ill patients appeared to function quite well in society. Despite their disabilities, they had friends and went to the movies, shopping, and so on. Other patients with similar problems remained at home, isolated from friends and family. The doctors hypothesized that the difference between the two groups of patients was in their psychological functioning and access to the resources that make life a little easier for everyone. As part of testing their hypothesis, they plan to give the two groups the Functional Status Inventory developed jointly by the Herbert Medical School and California University. After five years of study and validation, researchers at the two universities have prepared a survey on functioning for use with chronically ill patients. High scores mean good functioning; low scores mean poor functioning.

The methods used to produce an additive scale require sophisticated survey construction skills because you have to prove conclusively that high scorers are in actuality different from low scorers with respect to each and every item. When you use a survey that produces a single score, check to see if evidence is given that it means something.

Defining Additive Scales

Surveyors use the term *scale* in at least two ways. The first refers to the way the responses are organized:

1. Do you eat six or more servings of fruits or vegetables each day?

   The response scale is:

   Yes   1

   No   2

2. How satisfied are you with the examples in this book?

   The response scale is:

   Very satisfied   1

   Somewhat satisfied   2

   Somewhat dissatisfied   3

   Very dissatisfied   4

The second use of the term *scale* refers to one question or a collection of questions whose scores are meaningful. You have a quality-of-life scale when a survey with ten questions can be scored so that a score of 1 means low and a score of 10 means high quality.

Example: A Survey of Foreign Language Skills

Circle the category that best describes your ability to speak *each* of the following languages.

	Fluent	Somewhat Fluent	Not Fluent
French	2	1	0
German	2	1	0
Italian	2	1	0
Spanish	2	1	0
Swedish	2	1	0

For each item—French, German, and so on—an ordinal rating scale is used to organize responses. At the same time, by adding all five items together, a scale of language ability can be derived. A respondent who is fluent in all languages would be at one end of the scale, and one who is not fluent in any would be at the other. Suppose you assigned two points for each language marked "fluent," one point each for those marked "somewhat fluent," and no points for "not fluent." A person fluent in all five languages could get a maximum score of 10 points, whereas someone who was fluent in none would be assigned the minimum score of zero. In this book, this type of scale is called *additive* (because individual responses to items are combined). Among the most commonly used additive scales are the differential, summated, and cumulative.

Differential Scales

Differential scales distinguish among people in terms of whether they agree or disagree with experts. To create a differential scale for an idea such as equality of opportunity, for example, means assembling many statements (e.g., "qualified men and women should receive equal pay for equal work") and having experts rate each statement according to whether it was favorable to the idea. Next you compute the experts' average or median ratings for each statement. Then you ask respondents to agree or disagree with each statement. Their score is based on just those items the respondent agrees with. To get the respondent's score, you look at the experts' average score for each statement chosen by the respondent, add the experts' averages, and compute the arithmetic mean.

Typically, the directions to users of differential scales go something like this:

- Please check each statement with which you agree.

or

- Please check the items that are closest to your position.

Scoring a differential scale might take this form:

Example: Scoring a Differential Scale

Student A was administered the Physical Fitness Inventory and asked to select the two or three items with which she most closely agreed. These are the two items she chose and the judges' scores.

	Median Scores Assigned by Judges
1. Physical fitness is an idea whose time has come.	3.2
2. Regular exercise such as walking or bicycling is probably necessary for everyone.	4.0

Student A's score was 3.6 (the average of 3.2 and 4.0), which was considered to be supportive of physical fitness. (The best possible score was 1.0 and the worst was 11.0.)

Are there disadvantages to differential scales? Perhaps the most obvious one is in the amount of work needed to construct them. Also, you must take into account the attitudes and values of the judges whose ratings are used to anchor the scale and interpret the responses. The judges may be quite different from the people who might use the scale.

Summated Scales

A summated scale aligns people according to how their responses add up. Suppose a self-esteem questionnaire has a series of items that use the same rating scale (agree, neutral, disagree):

Example: Creating a Summated Scale for a Self-Esteem Survey

Directions: Check if you agree or disagree with each of the following statements.

Check one box for each statement.

Statement	Agree	Neither Agree Nor Disagree	Disagree
a. At times, I think I am no good at all.	☐	☐	☐
b. On the whole, I am satisfied with myself.	☐	☐	☐
c. I often feel very lonely.	☐	☐	☐
d. My social life is very complete.	☐	☐	☐
e. My friends admire my honesty.	☐	☐	☐

How would you compute a summative scale for this questionnaire? First, decide which items are favorable (in this case, b, d, and e) and which are not (a and c). Next, assign a numerical weight to each response category. You might do something like this:

Favorable = +1 point

Neutral = 0 points

Unfavorable = –1 point

A person's score would be the algebraic sum of his or her responses to five items. The answers Person X gave are shown in the example that follows.

Example: Scoring a Summated Scale

Statement	Person X's Response Disagree	Neither Agree nor Disagree	Agree	Is Item Favorable (+) or Unfavorable (–)?	Item Score
a. At times I think I am no good at all.	✓	——	——	–	+1
b. On the whole, I am satisfied with myself.	——	✓	——	+	0
c. I often feel very lonely.	——	——	✓	–	–1
d. My social life is very complete.	——	——	✓	+	+1
e. My friends admire my honesty.	——	✓	——	+	0

Person X disagreed with Item a, which is fundamentally unfavorable, and got a score of +1. For Item b, the person was neutral and so earned a score of 0. Item c produced agreement, but it was fundamentally unfavorable; Person X got a score of –1. There was agreement with Item d, resulting in a score of +1 and a neutral response to e, producing a score of 0.

Person X's summated scale score was +1 of a possible total of +5. (A perfect score of +5 would have come about if Person X answered: a = *disagree*; b = *agree*; c = *disagree*; d and e = *agree*.)

Likert type scales (such as *strongly agree, agree, neither agree nor disagree, disagree, strongly disagree*) are summative.

3

GETTING IT TOGETHER

Some Practical Concerns

OVERVIEW

How long should a survey be? A survey's length depends on what you need to know, when you need to know it, the amount of time respondents are willing to spend answering questions, and your resources.

The first question on a survey should be clearly connected to its purpose; objective questions come before subjective ones; move from the most familiar to the least, and follow the natural sequence of time; keep questions independent to avoid bias; put relatively easy questions at the end (particularly in long surveys), but put "sensitive" questions in the middle; avoid many items that look alike; and place questions logically.

To boost the response rates for self-administered questionnaires, plan in advance and monitor results. Consider sending respondents a letter before the survey begins and also at the time of the survey. You can do this via snail or e-mail. Propose to send survey results, keep questionnaires short, and think about offering incentives. Interviews require preparation and planning also. Interviewers need systematic, intensive training. Set up a system for monitoring the quality of the interviews over time.

You should pilot test your survey to see that it can be accessed and administered easily and according to plan. Your main goal is reliable and valid survey data. Reliability refers to the consistency of the information you get, and validity refers to the accuracy of the information.

One way to promote the reliability and validity of your survey is to base it on an already-validated survey, but be cautious. Ask for evidence of the survey's reliability and validity.

Predictive validity is a measure of the survey's ability to forecast performance; concurrent validity means that the survey and some other measure agree on outcome; content validity refers to the accuracy with which the questions represent the characteristics they are supposed to survey. Construct validity is experimentally obtained proof that a survey intended to measure a specific feeling, attitude, belief or behavior truly measures it.

A pilot test helps you design a reliable survey. When pilot testing, anticipate the actual circumstances in which the survey will be conducted, and make plans to handle them. Choose respondents similar to the ones who will eventually complete the survey, and enlist as many people as you can. For reliability, focus on the clarity of the questions and the general format of the survey.

Pilot testing bolsters reliability and validity because it can help you see that all topics are included and that sufficient variety in the responses is available—if people truly differ, your survey will pick up those differences.

Most public and private agencies that conduct surveys, research, and evaluation or that perform educational services have policies on informed consent and confidentiality. Online surveys have special privacy and confidentiality rules. Be prepared to explain the risks and benefits to respondents if they complete the survey.

LENGTH

The length of a survey depends on what you need to know and how many questions are necessary so that the resulting answers are credible. Another consideration is the respondents. How much time do they have available, and will they pay attention to the survey? Relatively young children, for example, may stay put for only a few minutes. You must consider your resources. A ten-minute telephone or face-to-face interview will cost less than an interview lasting 20 minutes. Online surveys can be given to tens of thousands of people with one click. The technical expertise needed to design Internet surveys is costly, however. Here are two situations illustrating how the circumstances under which a survey is conducted influences its length.

Example: How a Survey's Circumstances Can Influence Its Length

Situation 1: The local library wants to be sure that it continues to meet the needs of a changing community. In recent years, many more of its patrons are over 65 years of age, and a substantial percentage speak English as a second language. Among the library's concerns are the adequacy and relevance of their exhibits, newspapers, magazines, and other periodicals; programs featuring new books and writers; and special-interest collections concerned with issues such as health. A bilingual volunteer will be devoting two mornings and one afternoon a week for eight weeks to a 45-minute face-to-face interview with users of the library. A 50-item survey form has been designed for the purpose.

Situation 2: The neighborhood library also wants to be sure that its services are appropriate for a population that is increasingly older and non-English speaking. The city has decided that the neighborhood library is not the only library in the city that is changing in its needs and has agreed to sponsor a survey of its library patrons. To minimize the amount of time that librarians and patrons will have to spend on the survey, a ten-minute, six-item, self-administered questionnaire is prepared by the central library office. Four questions are asked about the adequacy of the library's collection of books and magazines, computer access, and special-interest collections; two questions ask about the respondent's educational background and income. To facilitate the survey's efficiency, questionnaires are obtainable at the checkout desk, completed at the library, and left with the local branch librarian who then sends them to the central office for analysis.

PUTTING QUESTIONS IN ORDER

All surveys should be preceded by an introduction, and the first set of questions should be related to the topic described in it. Look at this introduction and first question for a telephone interview.

Example: An Introduction to a Telephone Survey and Its First Question

Hello. I am calling from the California University. We are surveying people who live in student housing to find out whether it is a satisfactory place to live. Your name was selected at random from the housing registry, a directory of students who have voluntarily listed their telephone numbers. Our questionnaire will take no more than four minutes. You can interrupt me at any time. May I ask you the questions?

[If YES, continue. If NO, say thank you, express concern for bothering the person, and hang up.]

[Continue here.]

The first question asks you about your overall satisfaction with your apartment. Do you consider it *[read choices]*:

1. Definitely satisfactory
2. Probably satisfactory
3. Probably not satisfactory
4. Definitely not satisfactory

[DO NOT SAY] no opinion or don't know/wrong answer

The interviewer starts off by saying that questions will be asked about satisfaction with students' housing, and the first question calls for a rating of satisfaction. People sometimes respond best when the first questions ask for objective facts. Once they become used to the survey and more certain of its purposes, they are more likely to provide the answers to relatively subjective questions. Suppose you want to know about the success of a summer city cleanup program, for example. You might first begin by asking participants how they first heard about the program and how long they had been in it (two questions of fact), and then, ask how well they liked their job.

Questions should proceed from the most familiar to the least. In a survey of needs for health services, items can first be asked about the respondent's own needs for services, then the community's, the state's, and so on.

Questions of recall should also be organized according to their natural sequence. Do not ask very general questions: "When did you first become interested in jogging?" or "Why did you choose jogging over other physical exercise?" Instead, prompt the respondent and ask: "When you were in high school, did you have any interest in jogging? In college?"

Sometimes the answer to one question will affect the content of another. When this happens, the value of the questionnaire is seriously diminished. Look at this:

Example: Ordering Survey Questions

Which question should come first?

A. How much help does your adviser give you?

or

B. Which improvements do you want in your education?

Answer: Question B should come before Question A. If it does not, then adviser–student relations might be emphasized unduly simply because they had been mentioned.

How about this: Which question should come first?

Example: Ordering Survey Questions

A. How satisfied are you with the president's economic policy?

or

B. What is the quality of the president's leadership?

Answer: Question B should precede Question A because a person who is dissatisfied with the president's economic policy (and perhaps nothing else) might rate the quality of the president's leadership lower than otherwise.

Place relatively easy-to-answer questions at the end of a survey. When questionnaires are long or difficult, respondents may get tired and answer the last questions carelessly or not answer them at all. You can place demographic questions (age, income, gender, and other background characteristics) at the conclusion because these can be answered quickly.

Avoid many items that look alike. Twenty items, all of which ask the respondent to agree or disagree with statements, may lead to fatigue or boredom, and the respondent may give up. To minimize loss of interest, group questions and provide transitions that describe the format or topic:

Example: Providing Transitions

The next ten questions will ask if you agree or disagree with different planks of the Democratic Party platform.

Questions that are relatively sensitive should be placed toward the end. Topics such as grooming habits, religious views, and positions on controversial subjects such as abortion and gun control must be placed far enough along so there is reason to believe the respondent is willing to pay attention, but not so far that he or she is too fatigued to answer properly.

Finally, questions should appear in logical order. Do not switch from one topic to another unless you provide a transitional statement to help the respondent make sense of the order.

Here is a checklist of points to consider in selecting the order for the questions in your survey:

Checklist to Guide Question Order

✓ For any given topic, ask relatively objective questions before the subjective ones.

✓ Move from the most familiar to the least.

✓ Follow the natural sequence of time.

✓ See to it that all questions are independent.

✓ Relatively easy-to-answer questions should be asked at the end.

✓ Avoid many items that look alike.

✓ Sensitive questions should be placed well after the start of the survey but also well before its conclusion.

✓ Questions should be in logical order.

QUESTIONNAIRE FORMAT: AESTHETICS AND OTHER CONCERNS

A questionnaire's appearance is vitally important. A written self-administered questionnaire that is hard to read can confuse or irritate respondents. The result is loss of data. A poorly designed interview form with inadequate space for recording answers will reduce the efficiency of even the most skilled interviewers.

Here are some dos and don'ts:

Do: Put just one question on a line. Leave plenty of space for responses.

Don't: Squeeze several questions together. Do not abbreviate questions.

Response Format

The general rule is to leave enough space to make the appropriate marks. Here are several response formats.

Example: Response Formats

A.   ✓   1. Yes
           2. No
           3. Don't know

B. ① Yes
   2. No
   3. Don't know

C.   *Code*
  Yes   ①
  No   2.
  Don't know   3.

If you use the format shown as A, be careful to provide enough space so that this doesn't happen:

POOR:

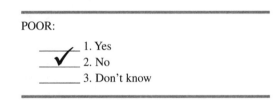

       1. Yes
  ✓   2. No
       3. Don't know

B or C is probably safer.

BRANCHING QUESTIONS, OR THE INFAMOUS "SKIP" PATTERN

What happens when you are concerned with getting answers to questions that you know are appropriate for only part of your group? Suppose you are doing a survey of young people's participation in after-school activities. You know that one major activity might be sports and another might be music, but you also know that only some participate in either.

If you want to ask about a topic that you know in advance will not be relevant to everyone in the survey, you might design a form such as the one in the following example.

Example: Skip Patterns or Branching Questions

3. Do you participate in sports?

  a. No (GO TO QUESTION 4)

  b. Yes

IF YES, which sports do you perform?

	Yes	*No*
Soccer	1	2
Track and field	1	2
Other. Please name	1	2

or

Do you participate in sports?

Yes   (Complete Section A)

or

No   (Go to Section B)

You must be extra careful in using branching questions (or as they are often called, skip patterns) in written self-administered questionnaires. In fact, some surveyors think that skip patterns are confusing to most people and should not be used in written questionnaires at all. Remember, respondents can skip important questions if they are baffled about where to go next on the survey form. Interviewers must be trained to follow the branches or else they might be unable to administer the survey correctly. Computer-assisted surveys (either online or on a laptop) are effective vehicles for branching because you can design the software to guide the respondent. For instance, if the survey instruction is, "If no, go to Question 6," the respondent who answers "no" will automatically be sent to Question 6.

ADMINISTRATION

Self-Administered Questionnaires

Self-administered questionnaires require a great deal of preparation and monitoring to get a reasonable response rate. These questionnaires are given directly to people for completion, and usually, very little assistance is available in case a respondent does not understand a question. A survey questionnaire asking about teachers' availability and needs for in-service training may be placed in his or her office mailbox, for example, with a week's return requested. Of course, teachers who have difficulty with the form might discuss the problem among themselves, but no guarantees

exist that the solution will be just as correct or incorrect as if the individual acted alone. Mailed and online questionnaires isolate the respondents most, because no one is usually available to clear up confusion.

Advance preparation, in the form of careful editing and tryouts, will unquestionably help produce a clear, readable self-administered questionnaire. To further ensure that you get what you need, you should review the returns. Are you getting the response rate you expected? Are all questions being answered? Here is a checklist for using self-administered questionnaires that can help you get what you need.

Checklist for Using Self-Administered Questionnaires

✓ Send respondents an advance letter via regular or e-mail telling them the purpose of your survey questionnaire. This should warn people that the survey is coming, explain why the respondents should answer the questions, and tell them about who is being surveyed.

✓ Prepare a short, formal explanation to accompany the questionnaire form. If you have already informed the respondent about the survey in a letter or via e-mail, you can keep this explanation short. It should again describe the survey aims and respondents.

✓ Offer to send respondents a summary of the findings. You can program online surveys to automatically display results. (If you promise this, budget for it.)

✓ If you ask questions that may be construed as personal—such as gender, race/ethnicity, age, or income—explain why the questions are necessary.

✓ Keep the questionnaire procedures simple. Provide stamped, self-addressed envelopes for mail surveys. Keep page folding to a minimum so respondents do not feel they are involved in complicated physical activities. You can provide direct links to the survey's URL for online surveys. Make sure people have easy access to their user name and login in case they forget.

✓ Keep questionnaires short. Ask only questions you are sure you need, and do not crowd them together. In written surveys, give respondents enough room to write and be sure each question is set apart from the next.

✓ Consider incentives. This may encourage people to respond. Incentives may range from money and stamps to pens, food, and free parking.

✓ Be prepared to follow up or send reminders. These should be brief and to the point. Do not forget to budget money and time for mailings and follow-up phone calls.

Interviews

Finding Interviewers. Interviewers should fit in as well as possible with respondents. They should avoid flamboyant clothes, haircuts, and so on. Sometimes it is a good idea to select interviewers who are similar to respondents. If you want to ask adolescent girls why they smoke, for example, you might hire young women to do the questioning.

It is also important that the interviewers be able to speak clearly and understandably. Unusual speech patterns or accents may provoke unnecessarily favorable or unfavorable reactions. The interviewer's way of talking is an extremely important consideration in the telephone interview. You should be keenly aware of the possibility that the interviewer's attitude toward the survey and respondent will influence the results. If the interviewer does not expect much and sends this message, the response rate will probably suffer. To make sure you are getting the most accurate data possible, you should monitor the interviewers.

Training Interviewers. The key to a good telephone or face-to-face interview is training, which should ensure that all interviewers know what is expected of them and that they ask all the questions in the same way, within the same amount of time.

Whether you are training 2 interviewers or 20, it is important to find a time to meet together. The advantage of meetings is that everyone can develop a standard vocabulary and share problems. If the trainees have to travel to reach you, you may have to think about paying for gasoline or other means of private or public transportation.

Once at the training site, trainees must have enough space to sit and write or perform any other activities you will require of them. If you want them to interview one another as practice for their real task, be sure the room is large enough so that two or more groups can speak without disturbing the others. You may even need several rooms.

If training takes more than an hour and a half, you should provide some form of refreshment. If you cannot afford to do that, at least give trainees time to obtain their own.

Trainees should be taken step by step through their tasks and given an opportunity to ask questions. It is also essential to tell them some of the reasons for their tasks so they can anticipate problems and be prepared to solve them. The most efficient way to make sure the trainees have all the information they need to perform their job is to prepare a manual. Here you can explain what they are to do and when, where, why, and how they are to do it. Consider setting up a group e-mail or designating a section of the project's Web site as a place to record changes in survey procedures and policies.

Conducting Interviews. Here are some tips on conducting interviews that should be emphasized in your training sessions:

1. Make a brief introductory statement that will describe who is conducting the interview ("Mary Doe for Armstrong Memorial Medical Center"), tell why the interview is being conducted ("to find out how satisfied you are with our hospitality program"), explain why the respondent is being called ("We're asking a random sample of people who were discharged from the hospital in the last two months"), and indicate whether or not answers will be kept confidential ("Your name will not be used without your written permission").

2. Try to impress the person being interviewed with the importance of the interview and of the answers. People are more likely to cooperate if they appreciate the importance of the subject matter. Do not try to deal with every complaint or criticism, but suggest that all answers will receive equal attention.

3. Prepare yourself to be flexible. Although it is important to stay on schedule and ask all the questions, a few people may have trouble hearing and understanding some of the questions. If that happens, slow down and repeat the question.

4. Interview people alone. The presence of another person may be distracting or a violation of privacy and therefore alter results.

5. If using a printed interview survey, be sure to ask questions as they appear in the interview schedule. It is important to ask everyone the same questions in the same way or the results will not be comparable. If using a laptop, you won't need to worry about the order of questions. You will have to learn what to do if the computer freezes or some other technical glitch occurs.

6. Interviewers should follow all instructions given at the training session and described on the interview form.

Monitoring Quality. To make sure you are getting the most accurate data possible, you should monitor the quality of the interviews. This might mean something as informal as having interviewers call you once a week or something as formal as having them submit to you a standardized checklist of activities they perform each day. If possible, you may actually want to go with an interviewer (if it is a face-to-face interview) or spend time with telephone interviewers to make sure that what they are doing is appropriate for the survey's purposes. To prevent problems, you might want to take some or all of the following steps:

- Establish a hot line—someone available to answer any questions that might occur immediately, even at the time of an interview.
- Provide written scripts for the interviewer. If interviewers are to introduce themselves or the survey, give them a script or set of topics to cover.
- Make sure you give out extra copies of all supplementary materials. If data collectors are to mail completed interviews back to you, for example, make sure to give them extra forms or disks and envelopes. As an option, consider having data collectors e-mail the results or enter them directly onto a secure Web site.
- Prepare an easy-to-read handout describing the survey.
- Provide a schedule and calendar so that interviewers can keep track of their progress. Numerous software programs are available to help you do this.
- Consider providing interviewers with visual aids. Visual aids may be extremely important when interviewing people whose ability to speak the language may not be as expert as is necessary to understand the survey. Visual aids are also very useful in clarifying ideas and

making sure that everybody is reacting to similar stimuli. For example, suppose you want to find out whether or not people perceived that the economy was improving. To ensure that everybody has access to the same set of data on the economy, you might show graphs and tables describing the economy taken from the local newspaper for the last one or two years. Another use of a visual aid might be in a survey of people's ideal expectations for a planned community. You might show several different plans and ask people to describe their reactions to each. The preparation of audiovisual aids for use in an interview is relatively expensive and requires that the interviewers be specially trained in using them.

- Consider the possibility that some interviewers may need to be retrained and make plans to do so.

THE SURVEY IS PUT ON TRIAL

Once your survey has been assembled, you must try it out to see that it can be administered and that you can get accurate data. That means testing the logistics of the survey (the ease with which the interviewers can record responses) as well as the survey form itself. The purpose of the trial (sometimes called a pretest or pilot test) is to answer these questions:

- Will the survey provide the needed information? Are certain words or questions redundant or misleading?
- Are the questions appropriate for the people who will be surveyed?
- Will information collectors be able to use the survey forms properly? Can they administer, collect, and report information using any written directions or special coding forms?
- Are the procedures standardized? If done in person, can everyone collect information in the same way?
- How consistent is the information obtained from the survey?

Reliability and Validity: The Quality of Your Survey

A ruler is considered to be a reliable instrument if it yields the same results every time it is used to measure the same object, assuming that the object itself has not changed. A yardstick showing that you are 6 feet 1 inch tall today and six months from today is reliable.

People change, of course. You may be more tired, angry, and tense today than you were yesterday. People also change because of their experiences or because they learned something new, but meaningful changes are not subject to random fluctuations. A reliable survey provides a consistent measure of important characteristics despite background fluctuations. It reflects the "true" score—one that is free from random errors.

A ruler is considered to be a valid instrument if it provides an accurate measure (free from error) of a person's height. But even if the ruler says you are 6 feet 1 inch tall today and six months from now (meaning it is reliable), it may be incorrect. This would occur if the ruler was not calibrated accurately, and you are really 5 feet 6 inches tall.

If you develop a survey that consists of nothing more than asking a hospital administrator how many beds are in a given ward and you get the same answer on at least two occasions, you would have an instrument that is reliable. But if you claim that the same survey measures the quality of medical care, you have a reliable survey of questionable validity. A valid survey is always a reliable one, but a reliable one is not always valid.

Ensuring Quality: Selecting Ready-to-Use Surveys

One way to make sure that you have a reliable and valid survey is to use one that someone else has prepared and demonstrated to be reliable and valid through careful testing. This is particularly important to remember if you want to survey attitudes, emotions, health status, quality of life, and moral values. These factors, and others like them, are elusive and difficult to measure. Producing a truly satisfactory survey of health, quality of life, and human emotions and preferences thus requires a large-scale and truly scientific experimental study.

Some surveys are available for purchase. To find them, consult the research literature. You do this by learning which online articles databases are appropriate for survey. For instance, to find surveys on children's reactions to community

violence, consider using a database such as PsycINFO. For educational measures, try ERIC. If your survey is health related, go to MEDLINE.

In reviewing a published survey (also in assessing the quality of a homemade form), you should ask the following questions about three types of reliability: test-retest, equivalence, and internal consistency.

First, does the survey have test-retest reliability? One way to estimate reliability is to see if someone taking the survey answers about the same on more than one occasion. Test-retest reliability is usually computed by administering a survey to the same group on two different occasions and then correlating the scores from one time to the next. A survey is considered reliable if the correlation between results is high; that is, people who have good (or poor) attitudes on the first occasion also have good (or poor) attitudes on the second occasion.

Second, are alternative forms equivalent? If two different forms of a survey are supposed to appraise the same attitude, you should make sure that people will score the same regardless of which one they take. If you want to use Form A of the survey as a premeasure, for example, and Form B as a postmeasure, check the equivalence of the two forms to make sure one is not different from the other.

Equivalence reliability can be computed by giving two or more forms of the same survey to the same group of people on the same day or by giving different forms of the survey to two or more groups that have been randomly selected. You determine equivalence by comparing the mean score and standard deviations of each form of the survey and by correlating the scores on each form with the scores on the other. If the various forms have almost the same means and standard deviations and they are highly correlated, then they have high equivalence reliability. Equivalence reliability coefficients should be high; look for those that are as close to perfect as possible.

Another measure of reliability is how internally consistent the questions on a survey are in measuring the characteristics, attitudes, or qualities that they are supposed to measure. To test for internal consistency, you calculate a statistic called coefficient alpha (or Cronbach's alpha, named for the person who first reported the statistic). Coefficient alpha describes how well different items complement each other in their measurement of the same quality or dimension.

Many surveyors are not at all concerned with internal consistency because they are not going to be using several items to measure one attitude or characteristic. Instead, they are interested in the responses to each item. Decide if your survey needs to consider internal consistency.

Example: Internal Consistency Counts

A ten-item interview is conducted to find out patients' satisfaction with medical care in hospitals. High scores mean much satisfaction; low scores mean little satisfaction. To what extent do the ten items each measure the same dimension of satisfaction with hospital care?

Example: Internal Consistency Does Not Count

A ten-item interview is conducted with patients as part of a study to find out how hospitals can improve. Eight items ask about potential changes in different services such as the type of food that might be served; the availability of doctors, nurses, or other health professionals, and so on. Two items ask patients for their age. Because this survey is concerned with views on improving eight very different services and with providing data on age and education of respondents, each item is independent of the others.

What is adequate reliability? The criterion depends on the purpose of the survey. To compare groups (say, employees at Company A with employees at Company B), reliability coefficients of .50 or above are acceptable. To make decisions about individual educational or health needs, you need coefficients of .90.

Here are some questions to ask about a published survey's validity:

- Does the survey have predictive validity? You can validate a survey by proving that it predicts an individual's ability to perform a given task or behave in a certain way. For example, a medical school entrance examination has predictive validity if it accurately forecasts performance in medical school. One way of

establishing predictive validity is to administer the survey to all students who want to enter medical school and compare these scores with their performance in school. If the two sets of scores show a high positive or negative correlation, the survey or instrument has predictive validity.

- Does the survey have concurrent validity? You can validate a survey by comparing it against a known and accepted measure. To establish the concurrent validity of a new survey of attitudes toward mathematics, you could administer the new survey and an already established, validated survey to the same group and compare the scores from both instruments. You can also administer just the new survey to the respondents and compare their scores on it to experts' judgment of the respondents' attitudes. A high correlation between the new survey and the criterion measure (the established survey or expert judgment) means concurrent validity. Remember, a concurrent validity study is valuable only if the criterion measure is valid.

- Does the survey have content validity? A survey can be validated by proving that its items or questions accurately represent the characteristics or attitudes they are intended to measure. A survey of political knowledge has content validity, for example, if it contains a reasonable sample of facts, words, ideas, and theories commonly used when discussing or reading about the political process. Content validity is usually established by referring to theories about personality, emotions, and behavior and by asking experts whether the items are representative samples of the attitudes and traits you want to survey.

- Does the survey have construct validity? Surveys can be validated by demonstrating that they measure a construct such as hostility or satisfaction. Construct validity is established experimentally by trying the survey on people whom the experts say do and do not exhibit the behavior associated with the construct. If the people whom the experts judge to have high degrees of hostility or satisfaction also obtain high scores on surveys designed to measure hostility or satisfaction, then the surveys are considered to have construct validity. This form of validity is usually established after years of experimentation and experience.

GUIDELINES FOR PILOT TESTING

Here are some basic rules for a fair trial of a survey.

1. Try to anticipate the actual circumstances in which the survey will be conducted and make plans to handle them. For interviews, this means reproducing the training manual and all forms; for mailed questionnaires, you have to produce any cover letters, return envelopes, and so on. For online surveys, you have to test the ease with which respondents can log on to a secure Web site and access the survey. Needless to say, this requires planning and time and can be costly.

2. You can start by trying out selected portions of the survey in a very informal fashion. Just the directions on a self-administered questionnaire might be tested first, for example, or the wording of several questions in an interview might be tested. You may also want to try out the survey process initially by using a different method from the one you eventually intend to use. So if you are planning to hand out questionnaires to conference participants, the trial may involve an interview so that any problems with the questions on the form can be discussed. In the end, you should give the survey logistics and form a fair pretrial.

3. Choose respondents similar to the ones who will eventually complete the survey. They should be approximately the same age, with similar education, and so on.

4. Enlist as many people in the trial as seems reasonable without wasting your resources. Probably fewer people will be needed to test a 5-item questionnaire than a 20-item one. Also, if you see that the survey needs little improvement, stop.

5. For reliability, focus on the clarity of the questions and the general format of the survey. Here is what to look for:

- Failure to answer questions
- Giving several answers to the same question
- Writing comments in the margins of written surveys

Any one of these is a signal that the questionnaire may be unreliable and needs revision. Are the choices in forced-choice questions mutually exclusive? Have you provided all possible alternatives? Is the questionnaire or interview language clear and unbiased? Do the directions and transitions make sense? Have you chosen the proper order for the questions? Is the questionnaire too long or hard to read? Does the interview take too long? (For instance, you planned for a 10-minute interview, but your pilot version takes 20.)

6. To help bolster validity, you should make sure that all relevant topics have been included in the survey (given your resources). For a survey of political attitudes, have you included all political parties? Controversial issues? What else must be included for your survey to have content validity? If you are not certain, check with other people, including the trial-run respondents. Does the survey have room for the expression of all views? Suppose you are surveying people to find out how religious they are. If you had proof in advance that all are very religious, you would not need a survey. Unless you can show that at least in theory you can distinguish the religious from the nonreligious, no one would believe the results. How do you fix this? In the trials, choose people you know are religious and those you know are not and give them the survey. Do their responses differ?

7. Test your ability to get a range of responses. If people truly differ in their views or feelings, will the survey capture those differences? Suppose your survey is of a suburban neighborhood's attitude toward a proposed new high-rise building development. You should administer the survey to people who are both for and against the building. This will help reveal your own biases in how questions are worded and, for closed-ended questions, might help you identify choices that people who feel strongly one way perceive as missing but that you might not have thought of.

Consider this:

> In a pilot of a survey of children's self-report health behaviors, respondents were asked how often they washed their hands after eating. All six children between 8 and 10 years of age answered "always" after being given the choices "always," "never," and "I don't know." The choices were changed to "almost always," "usually," and "almost never." With the new categories, the same six children changed their answers to two "almost always" and four "usually."

ETHICS, PRIVACY, AND CONFIDENTIALITY

Many people have become suspicious of surveys. They fear that the information they provide will be used inappropriately. Many techniques exist for protecting a person's privacy and ensuring that all information is confidential. The surveyor needs to reassure potential respondents that these techniques have been incorporated into each survey.

All complete written surveys should be kept in locked files, and only a limited number of staff should have access to them on a "need-to-know" basis. At the conclusion of data analysis, the surveys should be shredded. Furthermore, you can separate identifying information (e.g., names, birthdates, Social Security numbers) from survey responses by assigning codes to individuals and using the codes to link them to their responses. Finally, online survey takers can be permitted to assign their own identification names and password when logging into a survey.

The use of surveys and concern for ethical issues are completely interwoven. Surveys are conducted because of the need to know; ethical considerations protect the individual's right to privacy or even anonymity.

If your survey is for a public or private agency that is receiving federal funds, you should know that the federal government has specified the legal dimensions of informed consent, privacy, and confidentiality. These dimensions include the following:

- A fair explanation of the procedures to be followed and their purposes
- A description of any risks and benefits
- An offer to answer any inquiries
- An instruction that the person is free to withdraw consent and to discontinue participation without prejudice

Confidentiality is protected by the "Protection of Human Subjects" guidelines of the Code of Federal Regulations. Confidentiality refers to the safeguarding of any information about one person that is known by another. A surveyor who has names and addresses of people, even in coded or "de-identified" form, may not use this information to reveal identities. In many surveys, confidentiality is a real concern because complete anonymity is virtually impossible. A code number or even sometimes just a zip code can help lead to the survey respondent's identity.

If you work for a private agency, organization, or business, you should check the rules of informed consent and confidentiality. Is there a human subjects' protection committee or Institutional Review Board (IRB) whose approval you must get? If you are a student, check to see whether you can ask the questions you are planning. Also, you may be part of a larger project that has already received approval for its activities as long as it conforms to certain standards— among them, the informed consent of respondents.

Informed Consent

The consent form gives potential respondents sufficient written information to decide whether to complete a survey. Here is a list of contents to include in an informed consent form.

Contents of an Informed Consent Form

- A title such as "Consent to Participate in Survey."
- The title of the survey.
- The purpose of the survey.
- Procedures to be followed, including where the survey will take place and its durations.
- Potential risks and discomforts. These may include answering questions that are personal or being in a closed room for two hours.
- Potential benefits to respondents and society. These may include new knowledge or better information to develop programs or policies. Sometimes, the benefits are not yet really known.
- Payment for participation. Say how much participants will be paid, and if no payment is provided, say so.
- Confidentiality. If the respondent's name is to be kept confidential, describe coding procedures, who will have access to the surveys, and where the completed surveys will be kept. If information is to be shared with anyone one, state with whom. You may be required by law to reveal survey results.
- Participation and withdrawal. Can the participants withdraw at any time? What happens to them if they do? (For example, do they still retain any incentives? Will they still receive the same education, social benefits, or health care they came for?)
- Identification of surveyors. Who should be called if questions arise about the survey?

Privacy and the Internet

Some people are reluctant to complete online surveys or even connect to survey sites for fear that their privacy will be compromised. To guard against this, many organizations develop their own rules for reassuring respondents that privacy will be respected.

The U.S. Centers for Disease Control and Prevention (CDC) has a privacy policy that can be used as model. The full version can be found on their Web site (www.cdc.gov).

CDC Privacy Policy

Unless you provide additional information, CDC collects only the following information as you browse through the CDC Web site:

- The domain name and browser used to access the Internet;
- The date and time of the visit;
- The pages visited; and
- The address of the Web site you visited immediately prior to visiting the CDC site.

CDC collects this information for statistical purposes and for evaluating the CDC Web site to make it more useful to visitors.

If you send an e-mail message to CDC or complete a questionnaire, form, or other online survey found on the CDC Web site, CDC will maintain the information in accordance with applicable federal law.

CDC does not disclose, give, sell, or transfer any personal information about CDC Web site visitors unless required for law enforcement or otherwise required by law.

The CDC site is maintained by the U.S. government and is protected by various provisions of Title 18, U.S. Code. Violations of Title 18 are subject to criminal prosecution in federal court.

For site security purposes and to ensure that CDC's service remains available to all users, CDC employs software programs to identify unauthorized attempts to upload or change information, or otherwise cause damage.

Use of Cookies

Certain CDC Web pages use "cookies," which are small amounts of information stored by your Web browser software on your workstation. In most cases, this information is temporary in nature (called session cookies) and is deleted as soon as you leave the CDC Web site. The use of temporary cookies is solely for the purpose of allowing the user to interact with the CDC Web site in an effective manner. In a few cases, the CDC Web site uses cookies to store information for a longer period than the current session (persistent cookie). In those cases, the Web page is clearly noted and the user can choose not to use that Web page feature. As noted above, in no case does CDC disclose, give, sell, or transfer any personal information about CDC Web site visitors unless required for law enforcement or otherwise required by law.

If you are in doubt about the rules and regulations regarding the protection of privacy and confidentiality for survey respondents, you can learn more about the ethics of privacy in research from the U.S. Government Office for Human Research Protection (www.hhs.gov/ohrp).

A FAR-REACHING WORLD: SURVEYS, LANGUAGE, AND CULTURE

Many surveys are translated into different languages. If you plan on translating your survey, do not assume that you can automatically reword each question into the new language. Between the original language and the next language often lies a cultural gap. You may need to reword each survey question.

To avoid confusing people and even insulting them because you misunderstand their language or culture, you should follow a few simple guidelines. These involve enlisting the assistance of people who are fluent in the language (and its dialects) and pilot testing the survey with typical respondents. Follow these guidelines.

Guidelines for Translating Instruments

- Use fluent speakers to do the first translation. If you can, use native speakers. If you can afford it, find a professional translator. The art of translation is in the subtleties—words and phrases that take years and cultural immersion to learn. If you use fluent speakers, you will minimize the time needed to revise question wording and response choices.
- Try out the translated survey with three to five native speakers. Ask: What is this question asking you? Can you think of a better way to ask this question?

- Revise the survey with the help of the original translator.
- Translate the survey back into the original language. Use a different translator for this task. Does this "back translated" survey match the original version? If not, the two translators should work together to make them match.
- Try the resulting survey on a small group (5–10) of target respondents. If the two translators could not agree on wording, let the group decide.
- Revise the survey.
- Pilot test the survey.
- Produce a final version.

If you want to find out the respondents' backgrounds or their ethnicity, you should probably rely on existing questions rather than creating your own. The following question about ethnicity comes from the U.S. Census Bureau. Census surveys are available from the U.S. government electronically and by mail.

Example: Question About Ethnicity

ETHNICITY

Do you consider yourself to be Hispanic or Latino?

Hispanic or Latino	☐
Not Hispanic or Latino	☐

RACE

What race do you consider yourself to be?

American Indian or Alaska Native	☐
Asian	☐
Black or African American	☐
Native Hawaiian or Other Pacific Islander	☐
White	☐

4

SAMPLING

OVERVIEW

Should you survey everyone or just take a sample? The answer depends on how quickly you need results, if the credibility of the findings will suffer if someone or some group is left out, and your financial and technical resources.

Sampling can be divided into two categories. A probability sample is selected by an objective method (such as drawing names at random from a hat), and you can also calculate each person's chances of selection. Nonprobability samples are convenient: You select only those respondents who are nearby and willing and available to complete the survey.

Random sampling and stratified random sampling are two probability sampling methods. Random sampling gives everyone who is eligible to participate in the survey a fair chance of selection. But you may come up against a problem. Suppose you have a group of people you want to survey. With random sampling, just by chance, you may get all men (or all women). If you want a 50–50 split, random stratified sampling can solve your problem. With this method, you divide the total pool of eligible people into two groups or strata, with men in one group and women in the other. To ensure an even split, you draw an equal number of persons at random from each group. If you plan to use many groups, you will need a larger total sample than if you only have two groups of interest.

You can sample individuals or larger units such as schools, offices, and hospitals. These larger sampling units contain clusters (of students, employees, nurses, physicians, patients), so the technique is called cluster sampling. Cluster sampling is done because it is convenient. You can choose the units at random. If you do, you will have to use somewhat complex statistical methods to reconcile a relatively small number of sampling units (such as schools) and their larger number of analytic units (such as classrooms and students).

Nonprobability samples include systematic and convenience samples. In systematic samples, every nth (e.g., every 5th or 500th) unit (individuals, schools, factories) is selected from a list of units. If n is randomly selected, systematic sampling becomes like random sampling. In convenience sampling, you select everyone who is available when you need them *if* they meet the criteria for your survey (right age or reading level, voted in the last election, have lived in the community for at least one year, etc.). Other nonprobability sampling methods include snowball and quota sampling.

How large should a sample be? Relatively larger samples reduce sampling errors. If you want to evaluate the performance of two (or more) groups, statistical methods can guide you in selecting sample sizes large enough to detect differences between the groups—if differences actually exist. Statistical methods may also tell you how large a difference you can observe (and if you will be able to observe differences) with the sample size you have.

The response rate consists of the number of completed surveys divided by the number of surveys eligible for completion. To improve response rate, make sure that respondents can easily complete and submit the survey, train surveyors to administer surveys and follow-up, monitor the quality of survey administration, keep responses confidential, and provide respondents with incentives and rewards when possible and ethical.

SAMPLE SIZE AND RESPONSE RATE: WHO AND HOW MANY?

When you conduct a survey, do you have to include everyone? If you decide to sample, you must ask: How many people should be included? If your company has 1,000 employees and you want to survey just some of them, how do you decide how many people to include? Say you want to compare long- and short-term job satisfaction. Statistical methods can help you decide how many persons should be included each time (short- versus long-term) so that if a difference in satisfaction actually occurs over time, you will be able to detect it. Say you have three months to conduct the survey and think you can survey about 300 of the company's employees. Statistical methods can help you determine how much of an effect you can detect, given the size of the sample your resources allow you to assemble.

Suppose you want to find out if your neighbors will support a community vigilance program in which each household takes responsibility for watching at least one other house when the owners are away. Consider also that you define your community as having 1,000 homes. Do you need to include all households? If you do, will the program be more likely to work than otherwise? Here are some questions you should answer:

1. *How quickly are data needed?* Suppose a recent increase in house burglaries is the motivation for the survey and you want to get started immediately. If you wait to survey all 1,000 homes in your neighborhood, you may waste precious time.

2. *What type of survey is planned?* If you are going to use a telephone or mailed, e-mailed, or online survey, your survey will probably take less time than if you plan to interview people in their homes.

3. *What are your resources?* If they are limited, you have to select a survey method such as telephone interviewing rather home interviewing.

4. *How credible will your findings be?* If all 1,000 homes participate, then you will have no problem arguing that your survey is representative of the neighborhood. If only ten homes participate, you will run into a credibility problem.

5. *How familiar are you with sampling methods?* Sampling methods can be relatively simple or complex. National polls and large research studies use very sophisticated techniques that depend on the skills of statisticians and other trained experts. Other methods may be easier to implement, but the resulting sample may not be an accurate reflection of the larger population.

How do you select a sample? You can use probability or convenience sampling methods (also called nonprobability sampling).

A probability sample is selected objectively. An example would be the use of special software to randomly select winning lottery numbers. Statistical methods are available to calculate the probability that each person has of being chosen (or winning the lottery). A convenience or nonprobability sample includes people who are available and willing to take the survey. The sample selection process is not considered "objective" because not every eligible person has an equal chance. If you are ill on the day of the survey, you will not be able to participate even if you meet all other requirements.

Consider these two cases:

Example: Probability and Nonprobability Sampling

Case 1. A survey aims to find out how teachers in the Loeb School feel about certain school reforms. All 100 teachers' names are put into a hat, the names are jumbled, and the principal selects 50 for the survey.

Case 2. A survey is conducted to find out from teachers in the Los Hadas School district their views on certain school reforms. Ten teachers are chosen to be interviewed from each of the district's six elementary schools; 15 are selected from its four intermediate schools; and 60 are chosen from its one high school. Participating teachers are volunteers who were recommended by their principal. They meet the following criteria: They have been teaching in the district for five or more years, they belong to one of three teachers' associations or unions, and they have participated in at least one meeting during the past year on the district's school reform.

In the first survey, a sample of 50 of 100 teachers is chosen from a hat. This type of sampling is consistent with probability sampling because the selection method is objective, and you can use a mathematical formula to calculate the probability of each person's being selected. Also, you can usually expect that the two groups of teachers will not be systematically different from one another. In each group of 50, you are likely to have similar numbers of people who are smart, healthy, and generous and similar numbers who are not smart, unhealthy, and miserly.

In the second survey example, principals make recommendations, and eligible teachers voluntarily choose to participate. Principals may have their favorites. Teachers who volunteer may systematically differ from those who do not. They may be more enthusiastic about the survey or have more time to complete it, for example. This sampling strategy is not objective. It comes up with a nonprobability sample.

PROBABILITY SAMPLING METHODS

Three of the most commonly used probability sampling methods are the following:

- Simple random sampling
- Stratified random sampling
- Simple random cluster sampling

Simple Random Sampling

A simple random sample is one in which each person has an equal chance of being selected from a population. The population contains everyone who is eligible for the survey.

The following is simple random sampling:

Example: Simple Random Sampling

You want to select 100 people from philanthropic foundations to survey them about the types of grants they sponsor. A total of 400 people can provide this information. You place their names in any order. Each name is given a number from 001 to 400. Then, using a table of random numbers (found in statistics textbooks), you select the first 100 people whose numbers show up on the table.

Each person in this scenario has an equal opportunity for selection. The population consists of 400 people. Chance alone decides which of them is sampled.

The following is not random sampling:

Examples: Not Random Sampling

You want to sample 100 people from philanthropic foundations to survey them about the types of grants they sponsor. A total of 400 people can provide this information. You select 25 people in each of four areas of the country.

Some people in this scenario have no chance of selection: those who do not live in your four chosen geographic areas.

Here is another example of simple random sampling:

Example: Random Sampling

Two hundred nurses, therapists, and social workers employed by a Midwest city signed up for an adult day care seminar. The city had only enough money to pay for 50 participants. The seminar director used the random assignment feature in her statistics program software to select 50 names.

To facilitate simple random sampling for telephone surveys, some surveyors use a technique called random digit dialing. In one of its variations, called the plus-one approach, a digit is added to the telephone number that is actually selected. If the selected telephone number is 311-459-4231, the number called is 311-459-4232. This technique helps to make up for the fact that in many areas of the country, particularly in urban areas, people do not list their telephone numbers. These people are not fair shakes for selection for telephone surveys.

The advantages of simple random sampling are these:

- It is the simplest of all probability sampling methods.
- Aids are available to assist you. Most statistics textbooks have easy-to-use tables for drawing a random sample. An alternative is to use the random-number feature found in all statistical software.

A major disadvantage of random sampling is that it cannot be used to divide respondents into subgroups or strata (e.g., 60% male and 40% female). To make sure you have the proportions you need in a sample, you need to stratify.

Stratified Random Sampling

In simple random sampling, you choose a subset of respondents at random from a population. In stratified random sampling, you first subdivide the population into subgroups or strata and select a given number or proportion of respondents from each stratum to get a sample.

You can, for example, use stratified random sampling to get an equal representation of males and females. You do this by dividing the entire group into subgroups of males and females and then randomly choosing a given number of respondents from each subgroup. This method of sampling can be more precise than simple random sampling because it homogenizes the groups, but only if you choose the strata properly. That is, do not sample men and women unless you are planning to make comparisons between them. You should plan to make comparisons only if you have some reasons to believe, in advance, that those comparisons might be meaningful. In a survey of voter preference, for example, if you have some evidence that men and women vote differently, then it makes sense to be sure that your survey includes enough males and females to compare them. With random sampling alone, you might find that by chance you have a survey sample that consists mainly of men or mainly of women.

Here is how stratified random sampling works:

Example: Stratified Random Sampling

The University Health Center is considering the adoption of a new program to help young adults lose weight. Before changing programs, the administration commissioned a survey to find out, among other things, how their new program compared with the current one and how male and female students of different ages performed. Previous experience had suggested that older students appeared to do better in weight-reduction programs. The surveyors therefore planned to get a sample of men and women in two age groups; 17 to 22 years and 23 to 28 years and to compare their performance in each of the programs.

About 310 undergraduates signed up for the health center's regular weight-reduction program for the winter seminar. Of the 310, 140 were between 17 and 22 years old, and 62 of these were men. Some 170 students were between 23 and 28 years, and 80 of these were men. The surveyors randomly selected 40 persons from each of the four subgroups (male, female, aged 17 to 22, and aged 23 to 28) and randomly assigned every other student to the new program. The sample looked like this:

University Health Center's Weight-Loss Program

	Age 17–22 Years		Age 23–28 Years		
	Male	Female	Male	Female	Total
Regular program	20	20	20	20	80
New program	20	20	20	20	80
Totals	40	40	40	40	160

An advantage of stratified random sampling is that the surveyor can choose a sample that represents the various groups and patterns of characteristics in the desired proportions. The disadvantages of stratified random sampling are that it requires more effort than simple random sampling, and it often needs a larger sample size than a random sample to produce statistically meaningful results. Remember, for each stratum or subgroup, you probably need 20 to 30 persons to make meaningful statistical comparisons.

If you have difficulty selecting a stratified random sample, keep in mind that the same increase in precision obtained with stratification can generally be produced by increasing the sample size of a simple random sample. Increasing sample size may be easier than implementing a stratified random sample.

Simple Random Cluster Sampling

Simple random cluster sampling is used primarily for administrative convenience, not to improve sampling precision. Sometimes random selection of individuals simply cannot be used. For instance, it would interrupt every hospital ward to choose just a few patients from each ward for a survey. Sometimes random selection of individuals can be administratively impossible.

One solution to the problem of using individuals as a sampling unit is to use groups or clusters of respondents.

In simple random sampling, you randomly select a subset of respondents from all possible individuals who might take part in a survey. Cluster sampling is analogous to random sampling except that groups rather than individuals are assigned randomly. This method presupposes that the population is organized into natural or predefined clusters or groups. Here is how it works:

Example: Simple Random Cluster Sampling

The Community Mental Health Center has 40 separate family counseling groups, each with about 30 participants. The center's director noticed a decline in attendance in the last year and decided to try out an experimental program in which each individual would be tested and interviewed separately before beginning therapy. The program was very expensive, and the center could afford to finance only a 150-person program at first.

Randomly selecting individuals from all group members would have created friction and disturbed the integrity of some of the groups. Instead, a simple random cluster sampling plan was used in which five of the 30-member groups—150 people all together—were randomly selected to take part in the experimental program. Each group was treated as a cluster. At the end of the six months, the progress of the experimental program was compared with that of the traditional one.

The advantages of simple random cluster sampling are that it

- Can be used when selecting individuals randomly is inconvenient or unethical
- Simplifies survey administration

The disadvantage of simple random cluster sampling is that it requires complex statistical methods to reconcile sampling units (the hospital, street, school) and analytic units (patients, homeowners, students). That is, you are sampling by cluster (such as schools), but you are analyzing data from individuals (such as students).

Although in the example you have 150 people in the survey, you really have just five units (the five groups of 30 persons each) to study. Why can't you study each of the 150 persons individually? When people are in special groups—classes, clubs, organizations, neighborhoods—they tend to share similar characteristics and views. Studying each individual may be redundant because one person may be very similar to the next. You need a relatively large number of people for each cluster for this problem to become less noticeable. Just how large a number you need is a statistical issue.

Complex sampling strategies require an understanding of sampling statistics.

NONPROBABILITY SAMPLING METHODS

Nonprobability samples are often easier to assemble than probability samples. But gains in ease can be met with losses in generalizability.

Systematic Sampling

In systematic sampling, you pick a number, say 5, and select every fifth name on a list of names that represent the population. If a list contains 10,000 names and the surveyor wants a sample of 1,000, he or she must select every tenth name for the sample.

Suppose you have a list of 500 names from which you want to select 100 people. You can randomly select a number between 1 and 10. If you chose the number 3, you would begin with the third name on the list and count every fifth name after that. Your sample selection will result in the third name, eighth, thirteenth, and so on until you had 100 names. If you select the "start" number at random, systematic sampling resembles simple random sampling.

There is a danger in systematic sampling. Lists of people are sometimes arranged so that certain patterns can be uncovered, and if you use one of these lists, your sample will be subject to a bias imposed by the pattern. For instance, relatively few people in the United States have last names beginning with W, X, Y, and Z, and they may be underrepresented in a systematic sample. Here is another example. Suppose you are sampling classrooms so that you can survey students to find out about their attitudes toward school. Say also that the classrooms are arranged in this order:

Floor 1	1a	1b	1c
Floor 2	2a	2b	2c
.	.	.	.
.	.	.	.
.	.	.	.
Floor *N*	*N*a	*N*b	*N*c

Suppose also that you select every third class starting with 1a. The sample will consist of class-rooms 1a, 4a, 7a, and so on, to *N*a. The survey of attitudes toward school can be biased if each "a" corresponds to a location within the school that faces the lawn and is quiet, and the "b" and "c" classrooms face the sports arena and are noisy.

In considering the use of systematic sampling, carefully examine the list of potential respondents first. If you suspect bias because of the order or placement of sampling units (people, classrooms), use another sampling method.

Convenience Samples

A convenience sample is one that you get because people who are willing to complete the survey are also available when you need them. Say you want to find out whether the student health service was any good. You plan to interview 50 students. If you stand near the clinic entrance during the day, you can recruit each person walking in. When you have a complete set of 50 interviews, you have a convenience sample. Here are several sources of bias in this sample:

- Students who are willing to be interviewed may be more concerned with the health service than those who refuse.
- Students who use the service at the time of your interview may be going for convenience; sicker students may use the service at night.
- Students who talk to you may have a gripe and want to complain.
- Students who talk to you may be the most satisfied and want to brag.
- Students may want to talk but may have no time at the moment; these may be working students. Perhaps working students are different from other students (older?) in their needs and views.

Because of bias, convenience samples are unconvincing unless you prove otherwise. Here's how you might improve on the credibility of your convenience sample.

- Ask refusers and participants how concerned they are with their health and compare the responses. You may find no differences, and if so, then your convenience sample's findings are supported.

- Visit the clinic at night to find out if students using the health service then are different from the day students in their health status. You may find no differences. Again your sample is supported.
- Ask students if they have a gripe.
- Ask students about their satisfaction.
- Ask students why they refuse to participate. Is it because they presently do not have the time?
- Compare students who participate with those who do not in terms of age, gender, and so on. If no differences are found, your convenience sample's findings are easier to support than otherwise. If differences are found, you need to rethink your survey methodology.

Other Nonprobability Samples

Consider these common situations.

Example: Other Nonprobability Samples

1. A survey of 100 deans of law schools, senior partners in large law firms, and judges is conducted to find out to which lawyers they go to solve their own legal problems. The results are published in *Global News and World Reports* under the title *The World's Best Lawyers.*

2. What makes college students liberal or conservative? Family background? Region of the country in which they were born? Current religious practices? Educational attainment? Income? A survey is conducted of members of the Young Conservative Association and the Young Liberal Society. An assessment of the results reveals the reasons for students' views.

In the first example, the "top" lawyers may provide the services needed by deans, senior law firm partners, and judges. How applicable are the top lawyers' services to typical legal problems?

In the second example, students in only two organizations are being surveyed. Can we trust that they represent all students, including those who belong to other groups or choose not to join any?

These are standard nonprobability sampling techniques:

- *Systematic samples.* Every *N*th person or unit (school, hospital) is chosen.
- *Convenience samples.* Respondents are selected who are willing and available. The respondents may be individuals or clusters (the nearest ten schools).
- *Snowball samples.* Previously identified members of a group identify other members. For example, you select CEOs and ask them to nominate others.
- *Quota samples.* The group is divided into subgroups in specific proportions. This is similar to stratified sampling.
- *Focus groups.* Ten to 20 people are brought together to answer specific questions. A trained leader conducts the sessions. A transcriber is usually present to summarize the discussion.
- *Expert panels.* Ten to 20 persons are brought together to provide recommendations on controversial issues in health, social welfare, and education. Surveys are used as part of the consensus-building process.

FINDING THE SAMPLE

How do you find the sample? Before you look, you must decide who should be included (and excluded) from the survey. Suppose you want to evaluate the effectiveness of COMPULEARN, an Internet-based program to keep employees up to date on how to market products electronically. You decide to survey a sample of users and set these standards:

To be included in the survey, respondents must:

- Participate in the program for one or more months
- Be able to use FREENet software
- Be 30 years of age or older
- Read English

These eligibility criteria help you narrow your sample. But they do something else as well: They restrict your findings just to other people who also meet the standards. Here's why. After your survey is complete, you will be able to tell about the effectiveness of COMPULEARN only for persons who have been in the program for one or more months, who can use the specified software, and who are 30 years or older and English speaking. A person who is 29 and meets all other standards is by definition ineligible, and you will not be able to apply the survey's findings to 29-year-olds. (After all, you chose 30 years of age as an eligibility criterion because it presumably meant a critical demarcation point.)

Every time you do a survey, you must decide: Do I want to sample everyone or just people or places with certain characteristics? Usually the answer is "just people or places with certain characteristics (such as schools with 350 or more students)."

How do you get the names or list of persons or places to draw from? Try this:

How might you find the names, addresses, and telephone numbers of people in these two samples?

1. Plastic surgeons in California

2. Male high school English teachers in Barton School District

The plastic surgeons' names may be found on the Web in directories available from professional societies (the American Association of . . .). They may also be obtained by combing telephone books. You might be able to identify high school English teachers in Barton through the district's personnel records, their Web page, or by conducting a school-by-school survey.

Getting the list of potential respondents is often a complicated activity. To get the list, you are likely to be required to demonstrate your credibility as a surveyor and prove that you will respect the confidentiality of the responses. Once you have done all that, you then have to make certain the list is up to date.

Survey samples are obtained through advertising in offices, clinics, and via the media. You can also buy lists of names through special firms that specialize in maintaining databases.

How Large Should Your Sample Be?

Some surveys take place with just one group. A poll of a sample of voters is this type of survey sample. The trick is to select a sample that is "representative" of all voters who interest you. Other surveys are of two or more groups. For example, a survey comparing the career plans of students in the JOBS program with students in the CAREER program is this second sample. When comparing students' career plans, you may want representative samples of students in both groups. In addition, you have to think about the number of students you need in each of the two groups so that if a difference exists between them, you have enough "power" to detect it.

Consider these examples.

1. *Survey sampling: One group, no intervention or program:* You draw a sample from a population. You want to make certain the sample looks like the population.

> *Objective:* To survey mountain bicyclists 21 years and younger
>
> *Population:* Mountain bicyclists
>
> *Question:* How many mountain bicyclists do you need to make sure that your sample is a fair representation of mountain bike riders 21 years and younger?

2. *Survey sampling: Two or more groups and an intervention:* You have two groups. You want to compare them for differences after one of the two has been part of a new activity.

> *Objective:* To evaluate a chess program
>
> *Population:* Children who are in an experimental chess program and a control group of children who are not
>
> *Question:* How many children have to be in each group to detect a positive difference if one occurs?

When you think about sample size, you must also think about the standard error, a statistic used to describe sampling errors. Error exists because when you sample, you select from a larger population, and the sample typically differs from the population. This difference is a random result of sampling. You can control it but probably not eliminate it entirely. If you drew an infinite number of samples, the means would form a distribution that clusters around the true population value. This distribution, which has a bell shape, is the so-called normal distribution. In general, larger samples are more likely to collect around the true population mean and be a more accurate estimation of the population mean.

The Standard Error

Larger samples tend to reduce sampling errors when the samples are randomly selected. The statistic used to describe sampling error is called the standard error of the mean. It is the standard deviation of the distribution of sample estimates of means that could be formed if an infinite number of samples of a given size were drawn. Try this:

In a survey of 300 randomly selected respondents, 70% answer yes to the question: Is mountain bicycling one of your favorite sports? The surveyor reports that the sampling error is 9.2 percentage points. If you add 9.2 to 70%, or subtract 9.2 from 70%, you get an interval—called a confidence interval—that ranges between 60.8% and 79.2%. Using standard statistical methods, this means that the surveyor can estimate with 95% confidence that the "true" proportion of mountain bicyclers who answer yes falls within the interval.

The trick is keeping the confidence interval small. In practice, larger samples usually reduce sampling errors in random samples. But adding to the sample reduces the error a great deal more when the sample is small than when it is large. Also, different sampling methods (such as systematic sampling) may have different error rates from random sampling.

Remember that not all errors come from sampling. Although you want a large enough sample to keep the error low, you do not want sample size pressures to distract you so that other sources of errors blight your survey. Other sources of error include ambiguous eligibility criteria, badly designed and administered surveys, and poor returns.

Statistical Methods: Sampling for Two Groups and an Intervention

Suppose you want to compare two groups. First, divide the population in two (say, randomly). Then, use statistical calculations (such as the ones below) to find out if each group's sample size is large enough to pick up a difference,
if one is present. If the population is large, you may want to select a sample (say, at random) and then assign persons to the two groups. If you select a sample at random, you have random sampling. If you assign people to groups at random, you have random assignment. If you select all five schools in a city and randomly assign all students in each of the schools to groups, you have nonrandom cluster sampling and random assignment. If, however, you randomly select five schools in a city, assign three to an experiment and two to a control, and put all students in the experimental schools in the experiment, you then have random cluster sampling and nonrandom assignment.

Use the following checklist to get or evaluate a sample size when you have two groups and an intervention.

Example: Sample Size Calculations for Sampling Two Groups and an Intervention

✓ Assemble and clarify survey objectives and questions.

Decide the survey's purposes. Consider these:

Survey 1: Quality of Life

> *Objective:* To determine if younger and older women differ in their quality of life after surgery for breast cancer

> *Question:* Do younger and older women differ in their quality of life after surgery for breast cancer?

Survey 2: Anxiety in School

> *Objective:* To determine the nature and type of anxiety associated with school

> *Question:* Do boys and girls differ in their anxieties? How do younger and older students compare?

Each objective or question contains independent and dependent variables. Independent variables are used to predict or explain the dependent variables. They often consist of the groups (experimental or control, men or women) to which respondents belong or their characteristics (under 50 years old and 51 years of age and older). Take the question "Do boys and girls differ in their anxieties?" The grouping or independent variable is gender.

The dependent variables are the attitudes, attributes, behaviors, and knowledge the survey is measuring. In statistical terms, they are the variables for which estimates are to be made or inferences drawn. In the question "Do boys and girls differ in their anxieties?" the dependent variable is anxieties.

✓ Identify subgroups.

The subgroups refer to the groups whose survey results must be obtained in sufficient numbers for accurate conclusions. In the two surveys above, the subgroups can be identified by looking at the independent variables. Survey 1's subgroups are older and younger women. Survey 2's are older and younger boys and girls.

✓ Identify survey type and data collection needs.

The dependent variables tell you the content of the survey. For example, Survey 1's specific questions will ask respondents about various aspects of their quality of life. Survey 2's will ask about anxiety. Suppose Survey 1 is a face-to-face interview and Survey 2 is a self-administered questionnaire.

✓ Check the survey's resources and schedule.

A survey with many subgroups and measures will be more complex and costly than those with few. Consider this:

Subgroups, Measures, Resources, and Schedule

	Subgroup	Type of Survey	Comment
Survey 1: Do younger and older women differ in their quality of life after surgery for breast cancer?	Younger and older women: two subgroups	Face-to-face interview	May need time to hire and train different interviewers for younger and older women
			May have difficulty recruiting sufficient numbers of eligible younger or older women
Survey 2: Do boys and girls differ in their anxieties?	Boys and girls, younger and older: four subgroups	Self-administered questionnaire	May need time to translate the questionnaire from English into other languages
How do younger and older students compare?			Must develop methods to ensure confidentiality of responses

The number of subgroups ranges from two to four. Administering, scoring, and interpreting the survey for one group is difficult enough; with more than one, the difficulties mount.

✓ Calculate sample size.

Suppose a survey is concerned with finding out whether a flexible worktime program improves employee satisfaction. Suppose also that one survey objective is to compare the goals and aspirations of employees in the program with other nonparticipating employees. How large should each group of adolescents be? To answer this question, five other questions must be answered.

Five Questions to Ask When Determining Sample Size

1. What is the null hypothesis?

The null hypothesis (H_o) is a statement that no difference exists between the average or *mean* scores of two groups. For example, one null hypothesis for the survey of employee satisfaction is this:

> H_o = No difference exists between goals and satisfaction (as measured by average survey scores) between employees participating in the program and nonparticipating employees.

2. What is the desired level of significance (α level) related to the null hypothesis involving the mean in the population (μ_o)?

The level of significance, when chosen before the test is performed, is called the alpha value (denoted by the Greek letter alpha: α). The alpha gives the probability of rejecting the null hypothesis when it is actually true. Tradition keeps the alpha value small—.05, .01, or .001—to avoid rejecting a null hypothesis when it is true (and no difference exists between group means). The *p* value is the probability that an observed result (or result of a statistical test) is due to chance (rather than to participation in a program). It is calculated *after* the statistical test. If the *p* value is less than alpha, then the null is rejected.

When differences are found to exist between two groups, but in reality there are no differences, that is called an alpha or Type I error. When no differences are found between groups, although in reality there is a difference, that is termed a beta or Type II error.

3. What chance should there be of detecting an actual difference?

Power is the ability to detect a difference of a given size if the difference really exists. It is calculated as $1 - \beta$ (Greek letter beta). It is defined as the probability of rejecting the null hypothesis when it is false or of accepting the alternative hypothesis when it is true. You want high power.

4. What differences between means are important? That is, what is a meaningful $\mu_1 - \mu_2$?

Suppose the survey uses the Goals and Satisfaction Scale (GASS). This hypothetical scale has 50 points. If the scale is valid, you will have access to published scoring rules and data describing what the scores mean. Ask: Are higher scores better? How many "points" make a practical (educational or clinical) difference?

The answers to questions such as these will help you decide how much difference you want to detect in your two groups.

5. What is a good estimate of the standard deviation σ in the population?

The standard deviation (σ, lower-case Greek letter sigma) is a common measure of dispersion or spread of data about the mean.

If the distribution of values or observations is a bell-shaped or normal distribution, then 68% of the observations will fall between the mean ± 1 standard deviation; 95% of the observations, between ± 2 standard deviations; and 99% of the observations, between ± 3 standard deviations. Look at this:

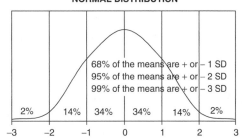

NORMAL DISTRIBUTION

68% of the means are + or – 1 SD
95% of the means are + or – 2 SD
99% of the means are + or – 3 SD

2%   14%   34%   34%   14%   2%

–3   –2   –1   0   1   2   3

Number of standard deviations from the mean

Estimates of the standard deviation can come from previously done surveys. Check that the sample used to derive the standard deviation is similar to your own. If it was not, the standard deviation in your group is likely to be different and so is your group.

Another way to estimate the standard deviation in your group is to conduct a small pilot test using about 25 to 50 people. You can also have experts give you estimates on the highest and lowest values or scores as the basis for calculating the standard deviation.

Below is one formula for calculating sample size for comparing the means from two independent groups (such as two groups of employees). Group 1 is in a program to improve satisfaction, but Group 2 is not. This formula assumes that the two groups' sample sizes and standard deviations are equal.

$$\frac{(z_\alpha - z_\beta)\,\sigma^2}{\mu_1 - \mu_2}$$

where

$\mu_1 - \mu_2$ is the magnitude of the difference to be detected between the two groups

z_α (the upper tail in the normal distribution) and z_β (the lower tail) are defined as

$$z_\alpha = \frac{X - \mu_1}{\sigma/\sqrt{n}} \quad \text{and} \quad z_\beta = \frac{X - \mu_2}{\sigma/\sqrt{n}}$$

Here is an example of how to apply the formula.

Example: Calculating Sample Size in a Survey of Employees in an Experimental and Control Group

Survey Situation. Devsoft's employees are participating in a program to improve their job satisfaction. At the conclusion of the three-year program, participants in the experimental and control group will be surveyed to find out about their goals and aspirations. The highest possible score on the survey is 100 points. The Type 1 or alpha level is set at .05. The probability of detecting a true difference is set at .80. A panel of experts in satisfaction measures says that the difference in scores between the experimental and control groups should be 10 points or more. Previous employee surveys found a standard deviation of 15 points.

The Calculations. For the calculation, assume that a standard normal distribution or z distribution is appropriate. The standard normal curve has a mean of 0 and a standard deviation of 1. (For more about the standard normal distribution, one- and two-tailed tests, and z values, see Chapter 6. Actual z values are obtainable in statistics books and program manuals.) The two-tailed z value related to $\alpha = .05$ is +1.96. For $\alpha = .01$, the two-tailed z value is 2.58; for $\alpha = .10$, 1.65; and for $\alpha = .20$, 1.28. The lower one-tailed z value related to β is –.84 (the critical value or z score separating the lower 20% of the z distribution from 80%). Applying the formula

$$(1.96 + 0.84)(15)^2 = 2\left(\frac{42}{10}\right)^2$$
$$= 2(17.64) \text{ or about } 36$$

At least 36 employees are needed in each group to have an 80% chance of detecting a difference in scores of 10 points.

Sometimes—for practical reasons—you can assemble only a certain number of persons for your survey. How do you know if the number is large enough to find differences? Again, statistics to the rescue. Look at this:

Example: Power to Detect Differences

The Alcohol Rehabilitation Unit has a program to reduce risks from alcohol use. It sets this standard of success:

At the end of the program, 20% of the harmful drinkers in the treatment group will reduce their risks, whereas 10% of the harmful drinkers in the control group will do so.

The unit hopes to be able to survey 150 persons in each group regarding their risks. Is this sample large enough? A statistician is called in to answer the question. The statistician produces this table for comparing percentage changes using a two-sided test with $\alpha = .05$.

N or Sample Size	%1	%2	Power
50	20	10	.29
100	20	10	.52
150	20	10	.69
200	20	10	.81
250	20	10	.89
300	20	10	.93

You interpret this table as follows:

"If we have 150 persons (final analytic sample size) in the experimental group and 150 in the control group, we will have 69% power to distinguish a shift of 20% in the experimental group from harmful to less risky from a shift of 10% in the control group."

You can use a statistical approach to distinguish different *effect sizes*. The effect size is the difference divided by the standard deviation. Look at this:

Example: 80% Power

The Alcohol Rehabilitation Unit will have complete survey data on 150 persons in an experimental group and 150 in a control. These persons will have completed a survey before they participate in the unit and immediately after. How much *power* will this sample size yield? Power is the ability to detect a difference or *effect*. Put another way, it is the ability of a statistical test to detect an alternative hypothesis of difference (between groups) of a specified size when the alternative is true (and the null is rejected). A statistician provides this table:

N or Sample Size	Effect Size
50	.56
100	.40
150	.32
200	.28
250	.25
300	.23

You interpret this table as follows:

"If we have 150 (final analytic sample size) in our experimental group and 150 in our control group, we will be able to distinguish a .32 effect size between the difference over time in the experimental group versus the difference over time in the control group."

Because you estimate effect by dividing the mean or average difference in scores by the standard deviation, you can see, for example, if the experimental group's mean improvement had a standard deviation of .50 and the control group's mean improvement had one of .10, then the effect size would be $50 - 10 = 40 > .32$. In this case, you will have at least 80% power to detect the difference of .40 between the treatment and control groups.

The preceding discussion is to assist you learn terminology and to aid you in evaluating the usefulness of your sampling methods and outcomes. *Sample sizes, effects*, and *power* are statistical terms. Unless you plan to learn statistics, call in an expert to help. Alternatively, consider using the sample size calculators found in statistical programs or on the Web. Go to your favorite search engine and type in "sample size" to find free sample-size calculators.

RESPONSE RATE

The response rate is the number of persons who respond (numerator) divided by the number of eligible respondents (denominator). If 100 people are eligible and 75 completed surveys are available for analysis, the response rate is 75%.

All surveys hope for a high response rate. No single rate is considered the standard, however. In some surveys, between 95% and 100% is expected; in others, 70% is adequate.

Here are some tips to improve the response rate:

Tips for Improving Response Rate

- Know your respondents. Make certain the questions are understandable to them, to the point, and not insensitive to their social and cultural values.
- Use trained personnel to recruit respondents and conduct surveys. Set up a quality assurance system for monitoring quality and retraining.
- Identify a larger number of eligible respondents than you need in case you do not get the sample size you need. Be careful to pay attention to the costs.
- Use surveys only when you are fairly certain that respondents are interested in the topic.
- Keep survey responses confidential or anonymous.
- Send reminders to nonresponders.
- Provide options for completing the survey. For instance, some people prefer online surveys; others prefer paper-and-pencil surveys that they complete and return by mail or fax.
- Provide gift or cash incentives.
- Be realistic about the eligibility criteria.
- Anticipate in advance the proportion of respondents who may not be able to participate because of survey circumstances (such as incorrect addresses) or by chance (they suddenly get ill).
- Tell respondents how you will use the survey's data.
- Be precise in describing how privacy is safeguarded.

5

SURVEY DESIGN

Environmental Control

OVERVIEW

A survey can be given to just one group or to many groups of people once or several times. For example, you can survey preschool children in one school just before and immediately after they participate in a new music program, or you can survey preschool children in ten schools just before they participate in the program and every two years after until they complete high school. A survey's design refers to its frequency (one time or more often), sequence (just before and immediately after), and the number of groups involved (all students in one school district or all students in each of ten districts).

A cross-sectional design provides a portrait of things as they are at a single point in time. Both a poll of voters' preferences one month before an election and a survey of the income and age of people who vote in a particular election use cross-sectional designs.

Longitudinal surveys are used to find out about change. Trend designs are longitudinal. When you survey one group of sixth graders in 2004, another group in 2006, and a third group in 2008, you have a trend design: trends among sixth graders. Another longitudinal design is the cohort. If you take a sample of children who were sixth graders in 2004 and in 2005 take another sample from the 2004 group, you are studying cohorts. A third longitudinal design is the panel. When you take a sample of 100 children who are sixth graders in 2005 and survey the same 100 in 2006, you have a panel design.

You may want to design a survey to compare two groups. Each group can be selected at random from a list of eligible participants, or you can take all who volunteer. Random assignment often makes it easier to draw valid conclusions from survey data.

A case control design is one in which groups of individuals are chosen because they have (the case) or do not have (the control) the condition being studied, and the groups are compared with respect to existing or past attitudes, habits, beliefs, or demographic factors judged to be of relevance to the causes of the condition. You have a case control design, for example, when you want to compare people who read a book a week or more with those who do not. Do they differ in education? Early childhood exposure to books in the home? Age?

WHICH DESIGNS ARE AVAILABLE?

Survey data can be used to describe the status of things, show change, and make comparisons. The survey's design refers to the way in which the "environment" is controlled or organized. The environment refers to the number and characteristics of respondents and how often and when they will be surveyed. The more environmental control you have, the more accurate your results will be.

The environmental variables over which surveyors have the most control are as follows: (1) when the survey is to be given (e.g., immediately after graduation); (2) how often (e.g., twice: immediately after graduation and 12 months after that; (3) the sample size (e.g., 10 or 1,000 graduates); and (4) the number of groups (e.g., just one, all graduates; or more than one, graduates of public schools and graduates of charter schools).

Look at these five surveys planned by the Have-A-Heart Association.

Example: Surveys With Differing Designs

1. The Have-A-Heart Association offers ten educational programs to people in the community. In June, it is conducting a survey of a random sample of people to find out and describe which of the ten programs they select and why.

2. The Have-A-Heart Association wants to know if people who participate in its educational programs gain knowledge about how to lessen their risk of a heart attack. The association conducted surveys with random selections of participants from programs offered in 2004, 2005, and 2006, and compared the results.

3. The Have-A-Heart Association has been concerned with monitoring community attitudes toward the role of proper diet in the prevention of heart disease. An educational campaign was launched in 1995. Every five years since then, the association has been monitoring attitudes by surveying a different random sample of people who were in the original program. This means that some people are surveyed more than once, and others are not surveyed at all.

4. The Have-A-Heart Association has been concerned with monitoring attitudes toward the role of a proper diet in the prevention of heart disease. An educational campaign was launched in 1995. Every five years since then, the association has been monitoring the attitudes of the same 500 people who were in the original program.

5. The Have-A-Heart Association has conducted an evaluation of the effectiveness of two competing programs that aim to reduce risks for heart disease through education. Participants were selected at random from the association's database. They were then randomly assigned to participate in one of the two programs. Participants' risks for heart disease were surveyed before program participation and 6 and 12 months after.

The first Have-a-Heart Association survey is to be conducted in June to describe the programs that the community selects. The design, in which data are collected at one point in time, is called cross-sectional.

The second association survey calls for collecting information over a three-year period and comparing each year's results with the others. This is called a longitudinal design and, specifically, a trend design.

For the third survey, the association will contact a different random sample of people from the original program. This design is called a cohort.

In the fourth survey, the same group provides respondents for a longitudinal study, and the design is called a panel.

The fifth association survey is used as part of an evaluation of the effectiveness of two programs. It uses a comparison group design.

Table 5.1 shows the relationship among the purposes, sampling and design concerns, results, and type of design for the five Have-A-Heart Association surveys.

CROSS-SECTIONAL SURVEY DESIGNS

With this design, data are collected at a single point in time. Think of a cross-sectional survey as a snapshot of a group of people or organizations.

Table 5.1   Relationships Among Purposes, Sampling and Design Concerns, Results, and Type of Design in Five Surveys Given by the Have-A-Heart Association

The Survey Is To Find Out About	*Concerns of Sampling*	*Concerns of Design*	*Outcomes*	*Type of Design*
Preferences for educational programs	A random sample of program graduates	When conducted: this year	Program selection	Cross-sectional
Knowledge acquired from educational programs	Different random samples of graduates	When conducted: 2004, 2005, 2006	Knowledge	Longitudinal: trend
Attitude toward diet in prevention of heart disease	Samples of randomly selected and possibly different graduates of the original program	When conducted: 1995, 2000, 2005, 2010	Attitude	Longitudinal: cohort
	Same sample of 500 program graduates	When conducted: Every five years	Attitude	Longitudinal: panel
The effectiveness of the program	Randomly selected from a database and then randomly assigned to programs	When conducted: Three times: before participation and 6 and 12 months after	Risks for heart disease How many groups: Two	Comparison

Suppose the Have-A-Heart Association wants to know which of its educational programs the community prefers. Consider this question and its answer.

Example: Cross-Sectional Design

Question: If only one program were possible, which would you choose?

Sample: A cross section of 500 people, randomly selected, who attended an education program this year

Design: Cross-sectional

Method: Telephone interviews

Answer: Dine-Out wins. Here is evidence in Tables 5.2 and 5.3.

Assuming that a sample of participants has been wisely chosen by a random sampling technique and the right questions have been asked, the tables in the example reveal that Dine-Out is the winner. This is why:

1. Regardless of gender or age, Dine-Out is ahead.

2. More men than women prefer Feel Fit and Emergency Care. But when it comes to Dine-Out, men and women have nearly the same preference.

3. People over 65 prefer Feel Fit, but there are not so many of them as people in the other two categories.

Of course, you might want to use only Table 5.1 or just Table 5.2 to make a point about your

Table 5.2   Educational Programs Preferred Most by Men and Women Participants

	Men		Women		Total	
	Number	Percentage	Number	Percentage	Number	Percentage
Dine-Out	168	34	175	35	357	69
Feel Fit	75	15	50	10	97	25
Emergency Care	21	4	11	2	46	6
Totals	264	53	236	47	500	100

Table 5.3   Educational Programs Preferred Most by Participants of Different Ages

	21–45		46–65		66+		Total	
	Number	Percentage	Number	Percentage	Number	Percentage	Number	Percentage
Dine Out	99	20	96	19	41	8	236	47
Feel Fit	35	7	37	7	90	18	162	32
Emergency Care	47	9	52	10	3	1	102	21
Totals	181	36	185	36	134	27	500	100

survey. You can also combine them into one large table. But a carefully planned cross-sectional design will give you a variety of ways for analyzing and presenting your survey data.

With this program preference data, for example, you might also have considered profession: How do people in business and the professions compare? Does retirement make a difference? Or residence: How do people in one part of the city compare with people in some other part?

Cross-sectional surveys have several advantages. First, they describe things as they are so that people can plan. If they are unhappy with the picture a cross-sectional survey reveals, they can change it. Cross-sectional surveys are also relatively easy to do. They are limited, however, in that if things change rapidly, the survey information will possibly become outdated.

Longitudinal Surveys

With longitudinal survey designs, data are collected over time. Longitudinal designs have three variations.

Trend Designs

A trend design means surveying a particular group (e.g., sixth graders) over time (say, once a year for three years). Of course, the first group of sixth graders will become seventh graders next year, so you are really sampling different groups of children. You are assuming that the information you need about sixth graders will remain relevant over the three-year period. Look at this example with participants in programs sponsored by the Have-A-Heart Association:

Example: Trend Design

Question: What do participants know about heart disease?

Sample: Random samples of 500 participants attending Dine-Out in 2004, 500 in 2005, and 500 in 2006

Design: Longitudinal, trend

Method: Self-administered questionnaires distributed and supervised by program instructors

Answer: In all three years, participants consistently know little about disease prevention, but by 2004 and 2005 they are beginning to learn about diet, and they appear to know the causes of heart disease by 2006.

Proof is displayed in the following table.

Participants' Knowledge of Heart Disease (N = 1,500)

	Cause of Disease	Nutrition	Prevention
2004	Little	Little	Little
2005	Some	Some	Little
2006	Much	Some	Little

SOURCE: Scores on the Heart Disease Information Scale, Health Survey Foundation, ©Los Angeles, 2003

As with cross-sectional studies, you could have analyzed the results of the heart disease knowledge survey by comparing men and women, different age groups, professions, and so on.

COHORT DESIGNS

In cohort designs, you study a particular group over time, but the people in the group may vary. Suppose, for example, you want to study certain people's attitudes toward diet as a means of preventing heart disease after they have participated in a special program sponsored by the Have-A-Heart Association.

You might survey a random sample of the program's participants in 2000, and then in 2005 choose a second random sample from the 2000 participants and survey them. Although the responses of the second sample might turn out to be entirely different from the first, you would still be describing the attitudes of the 2000 participants.

Think about this example, in which surveyors follow participants from a program first given in 2000 to find out about attitudes toward diet and how those attitudes changed over time.

Example: Cohort Design

Question: How have attitudes toward diet changed since 1990?

Sample: A different random sample of participants is surveyed every five years from among the graduates who participated in the Have-A-Heart Association program in 1990.

Design: Longitudinal, cohort

Method: Mailed self-administered questionnaires

Answer: In general, attitudes toward diet have improved since 1990. No relationship was found between gender and attitude, however. In 1990 and 1995, women had poorer attitudes (as measured by their lower scores) than men, but the situation was reversed in 2000 and 2005. For proof, see the figure below.

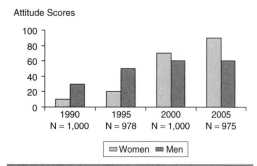

1990 Graduates' Dietary Attitudes

As can be seen from the figure, men's and women's attitudes fluctuated with time, although they both improved. What happened? Unless you systematically monitor the events that affect the graduates of the 1990 program, you will not be able to tell just by looking at the survey results.

PANEL DESIGNS

Panel designs mean collecting data from the same sample over time. If you were concerned with monitoring attitudes toward diet of male and female graduates of an educational program given in 1990, you would select a sample of participants and follow them and only them throughout the desired time period.

One way to display the results of your data might be as shown in the following example:

Example: Panel Design

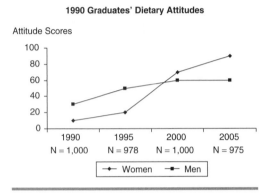

1990 Graduates' Dietary Attitudes

Attitude Scores

| | 1990 N = 1,000 | 1995 N = 978 | 2000 N = 1,000 | 2005 N = 975 |

Women   Men

COMPARISON GROUP SURVEY DESIGNS: QUASI- AND TRUE EXPERIMENTS

With these designs, people are divided into two or more groups, and their survey results are compared. The differences between the groups must be known before they are surveyed, or one of them must be part of a program to make them different. The classical comparison group design contrasts an "experimental" group with a "placebo" or "usual care" group. Consider this:

A. A survey is conducted of voters' preferences for candidates for the school board. As part of the analysis, men's and women's preferences are compared.

B. What is the relationship among frequency and type of exercise and severity of headaches? Two groups of people are identified. The first gets headaches frequently, whereas the second rarely or ever gets them. A survey is given to both groups to find out their exercise habits, and the results are compared.

C. How do you get people to participate in school board elections? A month before the elections, two groups of volunteers are assembled. The first

group is given a videotaped presentation, and the second is given a talk by prominent people in the community. After the election, the two groups are surveyed to compare the numbers who voted and to ask them to explain their reasons.

B and C use comparison group designs. The two groups in B were known in advance, and those in C were specifically created for comparison purposes. The design used in A is a cross-sectional one. A comparison is made between men and women from a snapshot of their preferences at one point in time.

Comparison group designs are sometimes divided into quasi- and true experimental designs. In quasi-experimental designs, assignment to groups is usually deliberate and not at all random. In true experimental designs (also known as randomized controlled) individuals may become members of one group or another: It is mainly a matter of chance. True experiments are the more powerful of the two.

Example: A Quasi-Experimental Design

You have been asked to evaluate two programs for the elderly. Eligible participants are assigned to the programs on a first-come, first-served basis, resulting in 60 people in Program 1 and 59 in Program 2. One of the issues addressed by a survey is whether the participants are satisfied with the staff of their program. To answer this question, you ask participants in both groups to complete a questionnaire at the end of three months' treatment. The design for this survey looks like this:

Attitudes Toward Staff
Participants in Two Programs for the Elderly

Program 1 *(N = 60)*	*Program 2* *(N = 59)*
Average attitude scores go here	Average attitude scores go here

DATA SOURCE: Scores on Attitude to Staff Questionnaire.

How valid is the quasi-experimental comparison group design used for the survey of the attitudes of the elderly in two programs toward their staff? Consider these possibilities:

1. Participants in the two groups may be different from one another at the beginning of the program. For example, older persons may choose one program over the other.

2. Participants who truly dislike the staff in one of the programs may have dropped out of the programs.

Example: A Quasi-Experimental Comparison Group and a Longitudinal Design

Another question posed for the evaluation of the two programs for the elderly is whether participants have learned about commonly prescribed drugs. To answer this question, participants have been interviewed at three times: at the beginning, at the end of the first month, and at the end of the first year. This survey design strategy can be depicted as follows:

Changes in Knowledge of Commonly Prescribed Pharmaceuticals in Two Programs

Time	Program 1 (N = 60)	Program 2 (N = 59)
Beginning of program	Interview results go here	Interview results go here
End of first month	Interview results go here	Interview results go here
End of year	Interview results go here	Interview results go here

DATA SOURCE: Interview with participants in each program.

The validity of this design may be threatened if persons with serious health problems are by chance more often assigned to one program over the other or by a different dropout rate from one group compared with the other.

Example: A True Experimental Comparison Group Design

The government commissioned a survey to determine which of three programs for the elderly was the most effective. Among the concerns was the cost of the programs. A comparison group design was used in which people at the Freda Smith Center were randomly assigned to one of three programs, and the costs of the three programs were compared. Program 1 had 101 people; Program 2, 103; and Program 3, 99.

A Comparison of the Costs of Three Programs for the Elderly at the Freda Smith Center

Program 1 (N = 101)	Program 2 (N = 103)	Program 3 (N = 99)
Average costs go here	Average costs go here	Average costs go here

DATA SOURCE: Interviews with financial experts.

NOTE: Participants were randomly assigned to programs.

This design is a relatively powerful one. Because people were randomly assigned to each program, any sources of change that might compete with the program's impact would affect all three groups equally. However, remember that although people were assigned randomly to the programs within the Freda Smith Center, other centers may differ, and therefore, the findings from the survey may not be applicable to other places.

Example: A True Experimental Comparison Group Design and a Longitudinal Design

Programs 1 and 2 in the Freda Smith Center proved to be equally cost-effective. The government then commissioned a study to determine which program was considered by participants to deliver the better medical care. To make the determination, a comparison group design was selected in which care was assessed from the beginning and end of the program and compared among people in Programs 1 and 2. The design is depicted by the following diagram.

A Comparison of the Medical Care Received by Participants in Two Programs for the Elderly

Time	Program 1 (N = 101)	Program 2 (N = 103)
Beginning of program		
Completion of program		

DATA SOURCE: The ABY Quality of Care Review System: surveys of doctors, nurses, patients.

This true-experimental and longitudinal design is among the most sophisticated and will enable you to make very sound inferences.

OTHER SURVEY DESIGNS: NORMATIVE AND CASE CONTROL

Two lesser-known survey designs are the normative and case control. Both offer some control over the survey's environment by making use of special comparison groups.

Normative Survey Design

A norm is a standard for comparing groups. Norms come from existing data or databases. For instance, norms are used when a particular school's reading scores are compared to a national average. Look at these:

Example 1: Normative Design

Participants in Los Angeles's Youth Program used the EFFICACY Survey, an instrument to measure self-efficacy that had been validated on a national sample of 5,000 people. The national sample was used as a norm, because there was no reason to believe that the L.A. group would differ from the rest of the nation in its self-efficacy. Youth Program scores were thus compared to those obtained by the national sample.

Example 2: Normative Design—Comparison to a Model

Are physicians in a new academic medical center as satisfied with their work as physicians in an older one? The new center has the same mission as the older one. To answer the question, physicians in both centers are surveyed and the new center is compared with the model older center.

Normative survey designs can be less expensive and time-consuming than other comparison designs. Remember, your group and the "normal" one may actually differ in important respects, resulting in less-than-valid findings. Suppose the participants in the Youth Program of Los Angeles were younger than the national sample, for example. If age and self-efficacy were related, with maturity associated with better survey scores, then the Youth Program would have to work harder to be a success. If you use normative designs, be prepared to defend your norm or standard for comparison.

Case Control Design

A case control design is one in which groups of individuals are selected because they have (the case) or do not have (the control) the condition being studied, and the groups are compared with respect to existing or past health care conditions, attitudes, habits, beliefs, or demographic factors judged to be of relevance to the causes of the condition.

Case control designs are generally used by researchers who are testing a specific hypothesis; for example, that a connection exists between lung cancer and cigarette smoking habits.

A case control design needs two groups: a case and the control. Ideally, the two groups should differ only in that the case has the characteristics or condition being studied and the control does not.

Most often, case control designs mean selecting a control that is like the case in ways that are strongly suspected to affect the condition. If you have evidence that gender affects frequency of headaches, then a study of people with headaches should have cases and controls with similar proportions of males and females.

The major weakness of case control design is that the two survey groups may not be alike at all no matter how selected or matched because of impossibility in controlling for all characteristics that may affect the condition. Some matching criteria might be incorrect, for example, or others may be excluded. Here is how a survey could be used with a case control design.

Example: Case Control Design

The University Medical Clinic randomly divided 10,000 patients between 21 and 55 years of age into two groups: those who had had a migraine in the past 12 months and those who had not. They used a stratified random sampling technique to select 100 people from each group, half of whom were female. A survey was conducted to find out about the following in relation to each group:

- Typical daily activities
- Potential sources of stress
- Family history and background
- Medical history
- Diet

6

ANALYZING AND
ORGANIZING DATA FROM SURVEYS

OVERVIEW

Some methods commonly used to analyze survey data include the following:

1. *Descriptive statistics*. These are the most commonly used analysis methods, and they are the basis for more advanced techniques.

2. *Correlations and regressions*. Correlations show relationships. A high correlation between height and weight, for example, suggests that taller people weigh more and that heavier people are taller. Regressions use correlations as the basis for predicting the value of one variable from the other. For example, suppose you want to know if being involved in high school athletics is associated with (or predicts) participation in college athletics. To find out, you would use regression analysis with your survey data.

3. *Differences*. Suppose you want to know if one group of respondents is different from another. Statistical methods used to test for differences in outcomes of surveys include the chi-square and *t* tests and analysis of variance.

4. *Risks and odds*. These analysis methods are used to describe the likelihood that a particular outcome will occur within a group, or they can be used to compare groups.

The appropriate analysis method for survey data depends on sample size, the survey's research design, and the characteristics and quality of the data. To choose a method, answer these seven questions:

1. How many people are you surveying?

2. Are you looking for relationships or predictions?

3. Will you be comparing groups?

4. Will your survey be conducted once or several times?

5. Are the data recorded as numbers and percentages or scores and averages?

6. How many independent and dependent variables interest you?

7. Are the data high quality?

Data management is an integral component of data analysis. It is the part of the analytic process in which data are entered into the computer so that you can get results. Do not underestimate the importance of this task.

Data management includes the preparation of a code book. The codes are the units that "speak" to the computer. To find out if coding is reliable, consider computing a statistic called the kappa. The kappa provides a measure of agreement between two coders.

Another key data management activity includes reviewing survey returns for missing data. Missing data results from unanswered questions or entire surveys. Data entry is the process of getting the survey's responses into the computer. Once data are entered, they need to be checked. A clean data set can be used by anyone to get the same results that you did. Data become "dirty" for a number of reasons, including miscoding, incorrect data entry, and missing responses. To avoid dirty data, make sure that coders or data enterers are experienced, well trained, and supervised. Alternatively, consider using online or scanned surveys that automatically "enter" data into a database.

WHAT IS TYPICAL ANYWAY? SOME COMMONLY USED METHODS FOR ANALYZING SURVEY DATA

The day has arrived. All the surveys have been returned. The response rate is high. All the questions and all the forms have been filled out. Now is the time to find out what the survey shows: How many men responded? Women? Do they differ? Have their views changed in the past five years? Surveyors answer questions like these by analyzing survey responses to obtain tallies and averages and to look for relationships, differences, and changes.

Some analysis methods commonly used in surveys include the following:

1. *Descriptive statistics.* These are the most commonly used, and they are the basis for more advanced techniques. Descriptive statistics for surveys include counts (numbers or frequencies); proportions (percentages); measures of central tendency (the mean, median, and mode); and measures of variation (range, standard deviation).

2. *Correlations and regressions.* These statistics show relationships. A high correlation between height and weight, for example, suggests that taller people weigh more and that heavier people are taller. A Spearman rank–order correlation is used with categorical data, those that come from categorical or ordinal scales. It provides you with a measure for the degree of association or equivalence between two sets of ranks, as in this example. Regressions use correlations as the basis for predicting the value of one variable from the other. For example, suppose you want to know if being involved in high school athletics is associated with (or predicts) participation in college athletics. To find out, you would use regression analysis with your survey data.

Example: Rank–Order Correlation

A class of 50 college students takes two attitude surveys. The first survey polls their views on universal health care, and the second asks about their political preferences. John scores highest (best attitude) among the respondents on one measure and average on the second; Jane's scores are the 5th and 8th highest; Bill's scores are the 14th and 13th; and so on. A rank–order correlation coefficient is computed to see if the two surveys agree: Do people who rank high on one also rank high on the other?

Pearson product–moment correlations are used to establish relationships between two sets of continuous data such as height and weight. Here are two situations in which these correlations are appropriately used:

- The relationship between grade point averages and scores on an attitude toward school survey are correlated.
- The relationship between liberal and conservative views (1 = *liberal* to 10 = *conservative*) and family income (from $5,000 to $50,000) are correlated.

Regressions are used to predict outcomes. Suppose you want to find out whether students who have high grades in high school are also likely to have high grades in college. In other words, you want to know if high grades in high school "predict" high grades in college. To find out, you would first survey college freshman to get their high school and freshman grade point averages. Then, you would examine the correlation between the two averages. Finally, you would survey a new set of high school students (who are college bound, but not there yet) and using regression techniques, "predict" their freshman GPA based on the original correlation.

Multiple regression techniques let you consider more than one predictor. Suppose you review the education literature and find that students who have high grade point averages in high school come from homes with relatively high household incomes. That is, the literature supports the hypothesis that a high correlation exists between household income and students' high school grade point average. You can now ask: What is the contribution of grades in high school (Predictor 1) *and* the contribution of high household income (Predictor 2) to college grade point average? A multiple regression analysis may be used to help you answer this question.

3. *Differences.* Suppose you want to know if one group of respondents is different from another. Are they healthier? More likely to vote in the next election? More employable? Better spellers? Statistical methods used to test for differences in outcomes of surveys include the chi-square test and ANOVA. Many of these methods actually hypothesize that the survey outcomes are the same across groups! The test of equality—the respondent groups are the same—is called the null hypothesis. Next, the statistical analysis is performed, a statistic is produced, and this serves as a guide in accepting or rejecting the null hypothesis. If the null is rejected in favor of an alternative hypothesis

(the groups are different), then the results are considered statistically significant.

Suppose you survey people on a cruise, half of whom are part of an experimental program combining tourism with education. You are fairly certain that the experiment is working. Nevertheless, you start out with the assumption that both groups are equally satisfied. Then, you compare the two groups' average satisfaction scores using a statistical method called an independent *t* test. You find that you are correct, so you reject the hypothesis of no difference. Because the average satisfaction scores of the experimental group were higher, you conclude that the experiment is working, you were right in the first place, and now you have statistics to back you up.

Here are some commonly used techniques for testing for differences among groups, or more precisely, testing whether or not they are the same.

Chi-Square

The chi-square is used with categorical data. It tests the hypothesis that proportions are equal. A proportion is what you get when you find out how many people of all possible people answer a certain way or have a specific characteristic. Suppose you sample 1,000 people and find that 250 have blue eyes. The proportion of people with blue eyes is 250/1,000. Suppose that of the 250 people with blue eyes, 60 are women. Suppose you want to compare the proportion of men (190/250) and women (60/250) with blue eyes. You have an idea that proportions are "significantly different" from one another. In other words, they are true and not chance differences. The statistical test you would use to compare the proportion is the chi-square. The symbol for chi-square is χ^2.

Example: Chi-Square

The Prison Organization surveys 60 imprisoned men and 40 imprisoned women to find out if they perceive the prison system as fair or unfair. The results are put in a table like this:

Perceptions of Prison System	Men	Women	Total
Fair	57	32	89
Unfair	3	8	11
Total	60	40	100

The table shows that 57 men and 32 women believe the system is fair, and 3 men and 8 women believe that it is unfair. The chi-square can be used to test the null ("no differences") hypothesis that the proportions of men and women are the same in their views of fairness. If the null is kept ("retained"), you conclude "no differences." The table is called a 2 × 2 table. The first "2" consists of the columns for men and women and the second "2" are the rows for fair and unfair. Chi-square tests can be expanded to include more rows and columns.

The *t* Test

The *t* test is also used to test for differences. It allows you to compare the average means of two groups to determine the probability that any differences between them are real and not due to chance. You should have at least 20 to 30 respondents per group and continuous data to use a *t* test. You need continuous data to calculate the arithmetic average or mean.

Example: *t* Test

Hope Hospital has initiated a gourmet meal plan. Charity Hospital says gourmet meals cost too much. Do the two hospitals differ in their patients' satisfaction with meals? The surveyors use the Satisfaction Scale (10 = *much satisfaction*, and 1 = *little satisfaction*). They also ask if any observed differences are statistically meaningful.

The Mann-Whitney U Test

The Mann-Whitney *U* test (also called the Wilcoxon rank sum) enables you to compare two independent groups when you cannot use the *t* test—say, because the sample size is too small. This statistical method is a test of the equality of the medians.

Example: Mann-Whitney U Test

Partridge Elementary School had ten fourth-grade students with severe hearing impairments. Four of the students were in a new program to teach them to speak

more clearly. At the end of one semester, students in the new program were compared with the six students in the traditional program. A special education expert rated each child's ability to speak on a scale from 1 to 20, with 20 representing clear speech. If more students had been available, the surveyor might have chosen the *t* test to compare the two groups, but after considering the small sample size, he decided to use the Mann-Whitney *U* test.

Analysis of Variance

Group means or averages can also be tested with analysis of variance (ANOVA). This method lets you test averages achieved by two or more groups. For instance, you can test for differences in average scores on a statewide test for students in Experimental School A versus Experimental School B versus Control School C.

Risks and Odds

Risks and odds are used to describe the likelihood that a particular outcome will occur within a group, or they can be used to compare groups. Suppose that for every 100 persons who have a cold, 20 people also have a cough. The risk of a cough with a cold is 20/100 or .20. The odds of having a cough with a cold is calculated by comparing the number of persons with (20) and without (80) coughs or 20/80, which is .25.

When you use risks and odds to compare groups, you compare the *relative* likelihood that an outcome will take place. The relative risk expresses the risk of a particular outcome in the experimental group relative to the risk of the outcome in the control group. The odds ratio is a description of the comparison of the odds of the outcome in the experimental group with the odds in the control group. You can use the relative risk or the odds ratio with 2 × 2 tables. Look at this:

Example: Odds Ratio and Relative Risk

Outcome	Experimental	Control
Still smoking		
Quit smoking		

You can ask: What are the odds of still smoking (or quitting) in the experimental group compared to the control? What is the risk of still smoking (or quitting) in the experimental group relative to the risk of still smoking (or quitting) in the control?

The relative risk and the odds ratio will be less than 1 when an outcome occurs less frequently in the experimental than in the control group. Similarly, both will be greater than 1 if the outcome occurs more frequently in the experimental than in the control group.

Why use the odds ratio or relative risk? Why not stay with chi-square? The answer is the confidence interval. Confidence intervals can be placed around odds ratios and relative risks (but not chi-squares), accomplishing the same objective as a significance test. That is, you can determine (by looking at the intervals) if the results are statistically significant.

4. *Changes.* Special forms of *t* tests and ANOVAs can be used to measure change over time. A dependent *t* test measures change in a single group from Time 1 to Time 2. Repeated measures of ANOVA can be used to detect changes in one or more groups at two or more times.

With the McNemar test, each person acts as his or her own control, and small samples and categorical data are used. For example, you can use a McNemar test to find out if a difference exists in number of students who do and do not choose careers in software engineering after they have participated in a counseling program.

PUTTING THE HORSE IN FRONT OF THE CART: SELECTING ANALYSIS METHODS

The appropriate analysis method for survey data depends on sample size, the survey's research design, and the characteristics and quality of the data. If someone asks, as people sometimes do, "What is the best method for analyzing survey data?", reply with seven questions that must be answered first.

1. *How many people are you surveying?* Sample size is an important consideration in selecting an analytic strategy. Some statistical methods (*t* tests and ANOVA) depend on

relatively larger samples than do some other methods such as the Mann-Whitney *U*. Look at these samples:

A. All 500 teachers in the school district.
B. A stratified sample of 50 teachers in the school district. The strata or divisions are men and women, and high school, junior high school, and elementary school teachers.
C. Six teachers in Hart senior high school and five in James senior high school.

Ask: Do you have sufficient data to compute more than tallies, averages, and the variation? You would for Example A, but you probably could not for Example C.

What about Example B? Suppose you were surveying a population of teachers of whom about 60% were women and 40% were men. If you took a sample of 50, and your stratification method was a success, you would have 30 (60% women × 50) in one group, and 20 (40% × 50) men in the other. Groups of 30 and 20 are just about large enough for a *t* test.

Consider this:

	Number of Teachers	
	Men	*Women*
Elementary	2	15
Middle School	3	10
High School	15	5
Total	20	30

If you want to compare men and women teachers in elementary school, you will have only 2 men and 15 women for your analysis (although for the total you have 20 men and 30 women). This leads to the second of the seven questions to ask when selecting analysis methods.

2. *Are you looking for relationships or associations?*

Example: Relationships and Associations

A. What is the relationship between voters' political views (as expressed on the Political View Survey) and number of years of formal schooling? The Political View Survey gives continuous scores ranging from 10 (liberal) to 100 (conservative).

B. Are high scores on the Political View Survey associated with high scores on the Authoritarian–Libertarian Inventory? How about medium and low scores?

In the first example, the degree of association between the two variables, political view scores and number of years of formal schooling, can be computed by using the Pearson product–moment correlation because continuous data are available. For the second example, with ranks of high, medium, and low, the Spearman rank–order correlation is appropriate.

3. *Will you be comparing groups?*

Example: Comparing Groups

A. Fifteen teachers in Hart High School will be compared with 20 in James Senior High.

B. A total of 100 male and females teacher from the district's high schools, junior high schools, and elementary schools will be surveyed in December and June and compared at both times.

If you are comparing groups, statistical tests such as the chi-square, Mann-Whitney U, t test, ANOVA, and McNemar tests can help you decide if any observed differences are due to some real occurrence or chance.

4. *Will your survey be conducted once or several times?* This question is to find out whether the survey design is cross-sectional or longitudinal.

Example: Looking for Change

A. All 500 teachers will be surveyed in December.

B. A sample of 100 teachers will be surveyed in December and again in June.

Here is a way to display the results of surveys conducted several times:

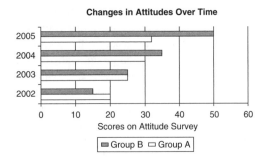

The graph shows that in 2002, Group B had lower scores than Group A. By 2004, Group B had passed Group A. Both groups increased their scores over time. Are the differences between groups significant? Are the differences over time significant? The graph cannot tell us. For statistical significance you need statistical methods.

Here is another way to display changes over time using the same data:

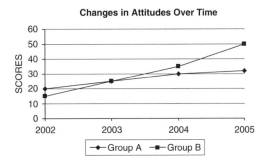

This line graph enables you to visually inspect the slope at which the scores changed. But like the bar graph, you cannot tell just from looking at the graph whether and to what extent the changes are significant.

5. *Are the data recorded as numbers and percentages or scores and averages?* Look at this:

A. One set of survey data consists of the number and percentage of teachers who agree or disagree with statements about the district's educational policies.

B. One set of data consists of scores on a measure of attitudes (liberal versus conservative) to various approaches toward education.

Survey data can be in numbers and percentages (categorical data) or scores that are amenable to the computation of averages (continuous data). The analytic techniques you use with each are different. Look at Tables 6.1 and 6.2.

Table 6.1   Comparing Men and Women Accepted Into Law School: The Numbers

	Coaching Program A (N = 102)		Coaching Program B (N = 206)	
	n	*(%)*	*n*	*(%)*
Men	50	(49)	100	(49)
Women	52	(51)	106	(51)

Table 6.2   Comparing Scores of Men and Women Accepted Into Law School: The Numbers

	Coaching Program A (N = 102)		Coaching Program B (N = 206)	
	X^a	SD^b	X	SD
Men	20.6[c]	2.3	42.8	2.9
Women	15.7	1.4	40.2	2.1

a. The mean.

b. The standard deviation.

c. Scores range from 10 = low to 50 = high.

Comparing numbers of people who were accepted into law school from different programs (categorical data) and comparing the mean scores on an attitude inventory (continuous data) require different analysis techniques. The first comparison might use the chi-square, for example, whereas the second might use a *t* test.

6. *How many independent and dependent variables interest you?*

A variable is a characteristic of interest to your survey. Health status, attitude toward school, self-efficacy, group (experimental, control), gender, job satisfaction, and quality of life are all variables. Independent variables are used to predict or explain findings. They usually include demographics (such as age, ethnicity, gender, income, and whether the respondent is in an experimental or control group). Dependent variables are what you are looking for in your survey: knowledge, attitudes, behavior.

Suppose you want to know if men and women differ in their quality of life. The independent variable is gender (men and women) and the dependent variable is quality of life. If you want to compare men and women in their quality of life and health status, you will have one independent variable (gender) and two dependent variables (quality of life and health status). You add an independent variable when you ask: How do men and women in the experimental and control teams compare in their quality of life and health status? The added independent variable is team (experimental and control).

You need to know the number of independent and dependent variables to select an appropriate analysis method. Listen to this:

Surveyor: I want to compare two groups of college seniors to find out their lifestyle preferences. There are over 300 in each group.

Analyst: What do you mean by lifestyle preferences? Are you planning to compare numbers of seniors who prefer certain styles of life—say, rural versus urban? Or are you comparing their scores on a survey?

Surveyor: Seniors in both groups have completed LIFEQUEST, a 100-item survey. It produces scores from 1 to 100. Higher scores represent more spiritual lifestyles, whereas lower ones mean more material ones.

Analyst: If you have scores on a continuum, you have continuous data. With two groups and continuous data, a *t* test sounds right.

Surveyor: What method would be correct if I decided to compare numbers?

Analyst: Chi-square.

Surveyor: Suppose I had more than two groups and continuous data?

Analyst: ANOVA.

7. *Are the data high quality?*

Data are high quality if the survey is reliable and valid, administered to the right number of the right people and recorded accurately. If the data are incomplete and untruthful, it probably does not matter which analysis method you use because the results won't mean much.

STATISTICAL SIGNIFICANCE

Suppose you survey the attitudes of two groups of students, one of which is in an experimental reading program. Also suppose that the experimental group's scores are much poorer than the other group's—say, by 10 points. Are the relatively poorer scores due to chance or is the new reading program responsible? Anything that is unlikely to happen by chance can be called statistically significant. How much of a difference between the two groups is necessary before you can eliminate chance as the motivation?

To determine statistical significance, you must rely on sampling theory. For example, you ask a question such as: What is the probability that my two random samples of students from the same population will produce mean scores that differ by as much as, say, 10 points? 20 points?

Suppose you decide that a chance happening of 1 time in 100 is an acceptable risk. This predefined probability ($p < .01$) is called the level of significance. If the differences you observe occur no more than 1 out of 100 times, you can reject the null hypothesis of no difference between groups.

Surveyors usually use the .05, .01, .001, and so on significance level, meaning that the observed difference in the experimental and traditional programs will be considered statistically significant if the difference of 10 points would occur by chance (assuming the two groups are random samples from the same population) only 5 times in 100, 1 time in 100, or 1 time in 1,000.

Understanding
Type I and Type II Errors

In testing statistical hypotheses, you must establish rules that determine when you will accept or reject a null hypothesis. The null hypothesis tests the proposition that the groups are the same or, put another way, no differences exist between (or among) groups.

Take, for example, a statistical test of an experimental (A) and control (B) reading program, where the null hypothesis is that the mean reading scores for both groups are equal.

When you apply a statistical test (such as the *t* test) to the data, you do not expect to find "zero differences" in mean scores between the two groups. Instead, the real question is whether the differences are so small that they could have occurred simply by chance. When you select two random samples from the same population, you can expect their mean scores to be close, but not exactly the same.

It is up to you to decide how far apart the scores must be before you are satisfied that the difference is not just an accident. You could choose .10, .05, .01, or .001 as the level of significance, depending on the amount of error you are willing to tolerate in rejecting the null hypothesis.

If you select the .05 level of significance, then about 5 times is 100 you will reject the null hypothesis when it is, in fact, correct. This happens because you are comparing two random samples from the same population, and the probability that they will differ by chance alone is 5% ($p < .05$). This situation is known as a Type I error. It is the probability of rejecting the null hypothesis when it is true.

If the level of significance is .01, then the probability of a Type I error is only 1 in 100, or 1%. You can select a level of significance that would virtually eliminate the chance of a Type I error, but there are serious consequences. The less likely you are to make a Type I error, the more likely you are to make a Type II error.

A Type II error is when you accept a null hypothesis that is, in fact, incorrect. In that case, the difference between the two groups' mean scores does not fall within the rejection region (say, $p < .05$). But in reality, the groups are not alike and the experimental treatment is better (the alternative hypothesis is true).

The power of a statistical test is the probability of correctly rejecting the null hypothesis. Mathematically, power is equal to Type I minus Type II error. From that formula, you can see that Type I errors, Type II errors, and power are interrelated. As the probability of making a Type I error goes down, the probability of making a

Type II error goes up, but the power of the statistical test goes down.

In statistical testing, you weigh the consequences and decide in advance on risk. Is it better to risk declaring the experimental group the victor when there is actually no difference between them (a Type I error)? Or is it better to risk saying there is no difference when the experimental group is really better (a Type II error)?

Because statistically significant results seem to be regarded as a research "finding" more often than insignificant results, Type I errors are more likely to find their way into print.

Confidence Intervals and *p* Values

Look at this portion of the results of an analysis of variance or ANOVA:

Example: Differences and Confidence Intervals

Group	Count	Mean	Standard Deviation	Standard Error	95% Conf Int for Mean		
1	7	11.0000	3.6056	3.6056	7.6654	to	14.3346
2	7	8.1429	4.2984	1.6245	4.1675	to	12.1182
3	7	16.4286	4.9828	1.0873	13.5123	to	19.3511
Total	21	11.8571	4.9828	1.0873	9.5890	to	14.1253

The results are in the form of a table with descriptive statistics: the number of units (the count), the mean, standard deviation, standard error, and the "Conf Int" or confidence interval for the mean. A confidence interval is a range of values within which the true value lies. So for Group 1, you can be confident that 95% of the time the true mean will be between 7.6654 and 14.3346.

You can plot the confidence intervals on a graph. If the means do not overlap, differences exist. If the mean of one group is contained in the interval of the second, differences do not exist. If the intervals overlap, but not the means, you cannot tell.

Look at this graph for the ANOVA confidence intervals.

Group 2's mean score is within Group 1's confidence interval. Group 3's interval does not overlap with either group. Differences in the means can be seen, and you can reject the null (that the means are the same). Also, notice that the *p* value (page) and confidence intervals agree in their outcome: The null should be rejected.

The confidence interval and *p* are related. If the interval contains 0, then the *p* is not significant. Confidence intervals are regularly used. In fact, they are often preferred in studies of two or more groups because you can see the range of values. A wide range is less conclusive than a narrow one. Compare an interval of means between 1 and 100 and one from 1 to 5. The wider range is less convincing.

A TECHNICAL INTERLUDE

Here are some common statistical techniques.

Tallies or Frequency Counts

A tally or frequency count is a computation of how many people fit into a category (e.g., 20 are over 55 years of age; 150 have a cold) or choose a response (e.g., 32 said definitely very important; 8 said more than three times a week).

Consider this:

Fifty preschools are surveyed. All are publicly supported. The following question was asked of each school director.

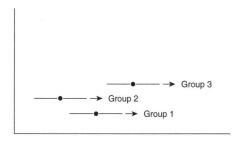

Group 1 Confidence Interval 7.67 to 14.33, $\bar{X} = 11.00$
Group 2 Confidence Interval 4.17 to 12.11, $\bar{X} = 8.14$
Group 3 Confidence Interval 13.51 to 19.35, $\bar{X} = 16.43$

Example: Preschool Purposes Questionnaire

Following are some possible objectives of preschool education. Circle how important each is in guiding your school's program.

Purposes	Definitely Important	Important	Neither Important nor Unimportant	Unimportant	Definitely Unimportant
To encourage creativity through music, dance, the arts	1	2	3	4	5
To foster academic achievement in reading, math, and science	1	2	3	4	5
To promote good citizenship	1	2	3	4	5
To enhance social and personal development	1	2	3	4	5

For the preschool purposes question, you can tally the responses as shown in the following example:

Example: Tallying Questionnaire Responses

Number and Percentage of Preschool Directors (N = 50) Choosing This Purpose

Purpose	N	%
Academic achievement	20	40
Creativity	13	26
Citizenship	11	22
Social and personal development	6	12

Tallies and frequencies take the form of numbers and percentages. Sometimes you want to group the responses together (or, in technical terms, prepare a frequency distribution of grouped responses), as shown in the next example:

Example: Grouped Ratings of Preschool Purposes by 50 Directors

Number of Directors Choosing This Purpose

Purpose	Definitely Important or Important N	Definitely Unimportant or Unimportant N
Academic achievement	40	0
Creativity	15	30
Citizenship	26	5
Social and personal development	7	42
Total	88	77

In this table, the responses are divided into two ("dichotomized"): important (including two categories of response: definitely important and important) and not important (including two categories of responses: definitely unimportant and unimportant). Why group responses together? If only a few respondents select one of the choices (say, only three answer definitely important), then the category may lose its meaning to you. Grouping may be confusing to the reader who may not know just how few people actually chose definitely important.

Averages: Means, Medians and Modes

The mean, median, and mode are all measures of average or typical performance.

The Mean. The arithmetic average, the mean, requires summing units and dividing by the number of units you have added together. Here are five scores: 50, 30, 24, 10, 6.

The average for these five scores is 50 + 30 + 24 + 10 + 6 divided by 5 = 24.

The formula for the mean is:

$$\mu_x = \frac{\Sigma X}{N}$$

μ is the symbol for the mean, and Σ stands for the sum, so ΣX means to add all the numerical values such as X. N stands for the number of Xs.

Suppose you wanted to compute the average rating for the four preschool purposes. First you'd have to know how many directors assigned each rating to each purpose (see Table 6.3).

Table 6.3   Ratings of 50 Preschool Directors

	Definitely Important	*Important*	*Neither Important nor Unimportant*	*Unimportant*	*Definitely Unimportant*
Academic achievement	26	20	4	0	0
Creativity	13	2	5	20	10
Citizenship	11	24	10	10	0
Social and personal development	6	1	1	30	12

To compute the average rating for each purpose, you would multiply the number of directors who chose each point on the scale times the value of the scale. For creativity, for example, 13 directors chose a 1, so you would multiple 13×1, add the results together $(13 \times 1) + (2 \times 2) + (5 \times 3) + (20 \times 4) + (10 \times 5)$ and divide by the number of directors: $13 + 4 + 15 + 80 + 50$ divided by $50 = 3.24$, the average rating for creativity.

In this case, the closer the averages are to 1, the more important the purpose (see Table 6.4).

Table 6.4   Average Importance Ratings Assigned by 50 Preschool Directors

Purpose	*Average*
Academic achievement	1.56
Citizenship	2.18
Creativity	3.24
Social and personal development	3.82

The Median. The median is the point on a scale that has an equal number of scores above and below it. Another way of putting it is that the median is at the 50th percentile. Because the median always falls in the middle, it is used when you want to describe "typical" performance.

Why do you need typical performance? Suppose you had a set of scores like this: 5, 5, 6, 6, 6, 8, 104.

The average is 20, the median is 6. How can this happen? It may if the group you were sampling was divided in its attitude (or knowledge or health, etc.), with most people feeling one way and some feeling much different. It can also happen if you are unable to collect all the data you plan to, and many of the people with one view are not represented in the responses.

Here is how to compute the median if you have an equal number of scores:

a. Arrange the scores in order of size.

b. Place the median between the $N/2$ score and the $(N/2) + 1$ score (where N equals the number of scores), using the arithmetic average.

Example: Computing the Median for Even Number of Scores

Take these scores: $-2, 0, 6, 7, 9, 9$.

There are six scores so $N = 6$, with $N/2 = 3$ and $(N/2) + 1 = 4$. The third score in order equals 6, and the fourth equals 7, so the median is 6.5.

Take these scores: 2, 4, 5, 8, 9, 11.

Again $N = 6$ so the median is between the third and fourth scores, 5 and 8. This time, however, there is a gap of three units between the third and fourth scores. Adding the two scores $5 + 8$ and dividing by 2 gives a value of 6.5 for the median.

When a set of data is small and odd in number:

a. Arrange the scores in order of size.

b. Place the median at the score that is the $(N + 1)/2$ from the bottom of the distribution.

Example: Computing the Median for an Odd Number of Scores

Try these: $-9, -8, -6, -6 -4, -3, -2, 0, 2$

The median of these nine scores is $(9 + 1)/2$ or the fifth score, and so the median is -4.

But suppose that in either an even-numbered or odd-numbered set of cases, you have several identical scores at the median or bordering it, as with this set: 3, 6, 7, 8, 8, 8, 9, 9, 10, 12.

When $N = 10$, as in this case, the median would usually fall between the fifth and sixth score. Calling 8 the median this time will not work because you need five different scores above and five different scores below.

But if you consider a score of 8 as part of a continuum that is evenly spread throughout the interval between 7.5 and 8.5, you can interpolate and come up with an intermediate score.

Think of it this way:

You have three cases (3, 6, 7) until you come to the interval of 7.5 to 8.5, which contains three 8s. Within that interval you will need two more cases to make a total of 5. So you add two thirds of the distance or .67 to 7.5, and you get a median of 8.17.

The Mode. The mode is a score (or a point on the score scale) that has a higher frequency than other scores in its vicinity. Look at these scores:

Distribution A		Distribution B	
Score	Frequency	Score	Frequency
34	2	34	0
33	6	33	1
32	8	32	7
31	11	31	11
30	15	30	4
29	18	29	3
28	16	28	7
27	12	27	10
26	8	26	18
25	3	25	123
24	1	24	11
23	0	23	5

Distribution A has a single mode of 29, with 18 people getting that score. This distribution is called unimodal. Distribution B has two modes, at 25 and 31, so the distribution is bimodal. (Although the frequency of 11 associated with the score of 31 is the same or lower than that of other scores, the score is a mode because it has a higher frequency than the others near it.)

The mode, with its concentration of scores, describes the prevailing view. You might use the mode when you suspect that you have a group with widely differing characteristics. For example, if you suspect that the reason people in Social Action Program D did better than those in Program C is because they were economically better off to begin with, you might compare their incomes before they entered each program.

If you find something like this, you could conclude that you are probably right.

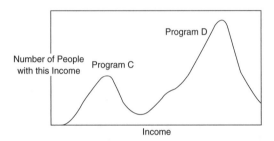

People in Program D are on the high-income part of the scale, while those in Program C are on the low-income side. Groups C and D together give you a bimodal distribution.

Variation: Range, Variance and Standard Deviation

When you compute an arithmetic average, every number counts. If one or two people have very high or low scores, they can make the average seem artificially higher or lower. Using the median helps, but it too can be misleading. Consider this set of scores: 2, 3, 4, 5, 6, 7, 8.

The mean and median are 5. If you were to change the last two scores to 17 and 18, the median would stay the same at 5, with three cases above and below the score, The mean would rise to 55/7 = 7.86.

If every number counts, it is sometimes important to study the spread of scores—their variation—to shed light on how the mean came to be what it is. Are all the scores near the arithmetic average? Are some very high or very low? Look at Table 6.5:

Table 6.5   Attendance at 60 Continuing
Education Classes

School	No. of Teachers	Average # Classes Attended	Range
1	50	55	16–60
2	103	54	53–60
3	86	41	15–59
4	117	47.5	15–60

If you look at the average number of classes attended at the four schools, you find that it is 47.5. Looking further, you see that at some schools, as few as 15 classes were attended, whereas at others, all 60 were. In fact, it is hard not to be struck by the range of attendance. At least several inferences can be made because you have access to the range.

1. Variation existed in three of the four schools (1, 3, and 4), with some teachers attending many classes and others attending very few.

2. In only one school (2) did almost everyone attend about the same number of classes as everyone else. In some cases, variation is considered an asset. A program to train people to think independently or creatively might expect a survey to reveal a variety of perspectives. You also need variation to make comparisons. If everyone performs equally well or shares the same views, you cannot select the best, the strongest, the most liberal or conservative, and so on. In other cases, however, variation is a disappointment because you want everyone to share the same view or achieve a skill at the same level of proficiency. If the district that is sponsoring the continuing education believes its programs are worthwhile, the wide range of attendance will be disappointing.

Another measure of variation is called the variance, and its square root is called the standard deviation. This is a statistical term based on a score's distance from the mean. In fact, the standard deviation is the average distance the average score is from the mean. Sometimes, instead of the standard deviation, the variance is used. The variance is simply the square of the standard deviation.

You can compute the variance and standard deviation on data only from continuous data such as average scores. Variation in categorical data (from categorical and ordinal scales) are best expressed in terms of the range.

Pearson Product–Moment Correlation Coefficient

Correlations measure the relationship between two variables. They are reported within a range of +1 (perfect positive correlation) to –1 (perfect negative correlation).

When high values on one variable occur simultaneously with high values on another, the two variables are said to be positively correlated, and when high values on one variable occur with low values on another, the two variables are said to be negatively correlated. The correlation coefficient is symbolized as *r* and is usually reported in two decimal places.

Warning: You can use correlations to identify relationships between variables, but you cannot use them to establish causation. Suppose you interview a sample of people to find out their highest level of completed education (Variable 1). You also ask them to tell you how many magazine they subscribe to this year (Variable 2). A correlation analysis can show that people who have completed many years of schooling subscribe to many magazines, but it cannot show that people subscribe because they had many years of schooling.

Analysis of Variance (ANOVA)

If you want to compare two or more groups or study changes that take place in the same group from one time to the next, ANOVA is a method you should consider. Here is how to proceed.

1. *Make Sure ANOVA Is Appropriate.* Remember, ANOVA is used to test for differences among groups or across times. Here are examples of questions that can be answered using one-way ANOVA:

- *Question* 1: Do patients in the experimental program have different mean satisfaction scores than do patients in the traditional program?
- *Question* 2: Do boys and girls in three different reading programs differ in their attitudes toward school? Attitude data are continuous and come from the ASQ (Attitude toward School Questionnaire).

2. *State Your Hypothesis.* In Question 1, for example, you will test the equality of experimental and control groups to learn about satisfaction. First you have to rephrase the questions as a hypothesis. You will be tempted to do this:

Tempting hypothesis: On the average, patients in the experimental program and patients in the traditional program are different in their mean satisfaction.

Preferred hypothesis: Patients in the experimental and control program are the same (or do not differ) in their mean satisfaction.

ANOVA cannot directly prove that there are differences among groups. It can only prove that they are not the same. To use ANOVA properly, you must test hypotheses about the sameness or equality of behavior and not the differences. The equality of means (remember in ANOVA, you test the equality of means) is called the null hypothesis.

3. *Make Sure You Have the Data You Need in the Form You Need.* ANOVA depends on the use of arithmetic averages and standard deviations. You cannot use ANOVA to test a hypothesis about the equality of two groups' behavior unless you have a way to determine their mean performance. This suggests that your survey uses scales that produce continuous data so that you can calculate the mean.

4. *Test the Hypotheses and Report the Results.* Hypotheses are tested with an F statistic, which is derived mathematically using the ANOVA formula. The null hypothesis for the F test is that group variances are equal. The variance is the standard deviation squared.

Look at the results for a sample ANOVA:

Example: Portion of a Results of a One-Way Analysis of Variance (ANOVA)

Page 3   STAT-PC 04/05/— ONE-WAY ANOVA

Source	DF	Sums of Squares	Mean Squares	F Ratio	F Prob.
Among groups	2	248.0000	124.0000	8.9793	.0020
Within groups[a]	18	248.5714			
Total	20	496.5714			

a. Some programs call this "Error"

These are sample results of a one-way ANOVA. The analysis is called one-way because there is only one independent variable (group), although there are three subgroups. Part 1 of the results includes a description of two sources of variation. Remember: The F test checks the equality of variances among groups (in this example, 3) and within each group. The F ratio is the statistic you get when you divide the among-groups mean square by the within-groups mean square (sometimes called the "error" variance). The F probability is the observed significance level: the probability of obtaining an F statistic as least as large as the one calculated when all population means are equal.

ANOVA compares the variation between each respondent and the respondent's group mean (within groups) and the variation between each group mean and the grand mean. The grand mean is the mean of all the individual group means. If Group A has a mean of 50 and Group B has a mean of 100, the grand mean is 50 plus 100 or 150 divided by 2, which is 75. If the observed probability is small enough, the hypothesis that all population means are equal can be rejected. With the probability of .0020 shown in the results, it is unlikely that the two groups are the same.

Notice that the ANOVA results give the F probability as .0020. All statistical programs automatically provide the exact p value such as .0020 (rather than $p < .01$) or .03 (rather than $p < .05$). It is recommended that you report the exact value of *p*. Like the confidence interval, it can provide additional and more precise information about the obtained difference.

t Test

The *t* distribution is used to test hypotheses about the mean (so you need continuous data). The shape of the *t* distribution approaches the shape of a standard normal distribution as its sample size approaches 30. A standard normal distribution is bell shaped. A typical normal distribution has a mean of 0 and a standard deviation of 1.

Here are three situations in which a *t* test may be used.

Example: *t* Test in Three Situations

1. *Client Satisfaction*

Employees at the Internext Network have scored a mean of 35.6. How does this compare to WorldOver's mean score? To make the comparison between groups, use an independent *t* test.

2. *Food Preferences*

Do average scores on the Good Food Inventory change after patients participate in a cholesterol-lowering program? To compare patients before and after they participate in the program, use a dependent *t* test.

3. *Clothing Prices*

The Price Survey found that women in the county of Thousand Palms spend an average of $150 each time they shop for clothing. How does this average compare with the national survey results? To compare the means obtained by women in Thousand Palms and the national means, use a one-sample *t* test. In this survey, the mean of a group is compared with a norm or standard: the national results.

A *t* test must meet certain assumptions to be used. For the independent *t* test, you need to satisfy two. Remember: An independent *t* test hypothesizes no difference between two groups whose survey results are given as continuous data. The first assumption to be fulfilled is that the data are normally distributed. How do you find out if the data are normal? The good news is that many computer programs will plot survey data for you so you can make this determination visually. But the data also need to meet a second assumption: The variances of the two samples also must be equal. The *F* statistic (same as the one for ANOVA) is used to test this assumption. Again, your statistical program will automatically give these results.

If the data do not meet these assumptions, you can "transform" the data or change its scale, or consider using nonparametric statistical methods that do not make assumptions about the distribution. The method to use to test for the difference between two paired samples is the Wilcoxon signed-ranks test. It actually tests the hypothesis that the medians (not the means) are equal. If you have independent samples, use the Wilcoxon rank-sum Test (also called the Mann-Whitney *U*). It also tests the equality of the medians.

Here is an example of the results of an independent samples *t* test.

Example: Independent Samples *t* Test

Global Tech is concerned that its employees are not participating in the firm's preventive health care activities as often as they should. Absenteeism is on the rise slightly, and Global is concerned that it may be health-related but preventable. The Human Resources Department conducts a survey to compare employees who use the Fitness Center more than once a week with those who use it once a week or less. The survey focuses on perceptions of physical health and well-being.

Type of Survey: Online survey

Survey Questions

- How often in the past 12 months did you use the Fitness Center?

  Once a week or less (yes, no)

  More than once a week (yes, no)

- The Physical Functioning Inventory (PFI) has ten questions. A score of 100 means highest physical functioning.

  Distribution: Normal

  Independent variable: Use of the Center (more than once a week versus once a week or less)

  Dependent variable: Physical functioning (score on the PFI)

  Analysis method: t test

  Results:

Page 3 STATUS+ 6/13/—

Independent Samples of Q41L — USE CENTER

Group 1: Q41 1.00[a] *Group 2: 2.00[b]*

t test for PFI scores:

	Number of Cases[c]	Mean[d]	Standard Deviation[e]	Standard Error[f]
Group 1	561	75.5261	23.957	1.011
Group 2	311	77.4358	24.112	1.367

	Pooled Variance Estimate[h]			Separate Variance Estimate[i]			
F Value[g]	2-Tail Probability[h]	t value	Degrees of Freedom	2-Tail Probability	t value	Degrees of Freedom	2-Tail Probability
1.01	.890	−1.13	870	261	−1.12	636.61	.262

Interpretation:

a. Group 1 chose "yes": Used the Center more than once a week. Their code is 1.00 for this group.

b. Group 2 answered "yes": Used the Center once a week or less. Their code is 2.00.

c. The number of cases refers to the number of employees who answered the survey (sample size) in each group.

d. The mean score obtained on the PFI by each group.

e. The standard deviation of the scores.

f. The standard error of the means.

g. The *F* value or statistic obtained in the test to determine the equality of the variances.

h. The probability of obtaining a result like the *F* value if the null (no difference between groups) is true. If the obtained probability is less than some agreed-on alpha such as .05 or. 01, the null is rejected. In this case, the probability of .890 is greater than .05, so the null is retained. The conclusion is that no differences exist in the variances of the two groups.

i. The pooled variance estimate is used when variances are equal. The *p* value is .261, greater than an alpha of .05. The null hypothesis regarding the equality of the group means is retained.

j. The separate variance is used when variances are not equal.

Conclusion

No differences exist in physical functioning between employees who use the Center more than once a week in the past 12 months and those who use it once a week or less.

Chi-Square (χ^2) for Two Independent Samples

This is an example of chi-square in use:

Example: Chi-Square

MEDEX is a program designed to encourage high school students to pursue careers in health. The school board commissioned an evaluation to see if MEDEX was a success. As part of the evaluation, 210 high school seniors were randomly selected and half received MEDEX and the other half did not. All 210 students were then surveyed at the end of the school year to learn about their vocational preferences. At that time, two of the students in the no-MEDEX group were disqualified from the evaluation when they enrolled in another program similar to MEDEX.

The evaluators organized the data into a table and used a chi-square statistic to test whether interest in careers in health was the same in both groups.

Group 1	Group 2	Total
A	B	A + B
C	D	C + D
A + C	B + D	$n = A + C + B + D$

This is a formula you can use for this 2 × 2 table:

$$\chi^2 = \frac{n\,(A \times D) - (B \times C)^2}{(A + B)\,(C + D)\,(A + C)\,(B + D)}$$

The formula was applied to the MEDEX Experiment:

No MEDEX	MEDEX
103	105

Career Preference	No MEDEX	MEDEX	Totals
No health	80	30	110
Health	23	75	98
Totals	103	105	208

$$\chi^2 = \frac{208\,[(80 \times 75) - (23 \times 30)]^2}{(103)\,(105)\,(110)\,(98)}$$

$$= 48.35$$

The evaluators used a table in a statistics textbook to determine the significance of a chi-square value of 48.35 with 1 degree of freedom (which you automatically get with a two-by-two design). The table gives the distribution of χ^2; the differences between groups were found to be statistically significant at the .01 level. The evaluators concluded that participating in MEDEX probably makes a difference in encouraging students to consider careers in health.

DATA ORGANIZATION OR MANAGEMENT

What is the best way to make sure the data are complete, reliable, and ready for analysis, interpretation, and reporting? Answering this question means learning about data organization or management.

Organizing or managing (as it is often called) survey data is an essential part of data analysis. It is the part of the analytic process in which data are entered into the computer so that you can get results. But before data can be entered, you have to decide how to prepare them so that you get the information you need in a useable form.

CREATING A CODE BOOK

The **codes** are the units that are used to "speak" to a computer. Suppose 5,200 college students complete an alcohol use survey called the College Alcohol-Related Problems Survey (CARPS). One question of concern to you is how many males report drinking five drinks at one sitting every day. To find this out, you have to tell the computer which variables to look for (e.g., gender and quantity and frequency of alcohol use). You also have to tell the computer how to distinguish males from females and how to come up with a number that represent how much each person drinks and how often.

Computer programs read about variables such as gender and quantity/frequency through codes. Look at this excerpt from the CARPS.

Example: Excerpts From the Computerized Alcohol-Related Problems Survey (CARPS), a Survey to Detect Binge Drinking in College Students

1. Are you male or female? [SEX]
    Male $\square_0$

    Female $\square_1$

    .

    ..

8. How often in the past 12 months have you had four or more drinks of alcohol at one sitting? [QFDRINK]

    Choose one answer

    Daily or almost daily
    $\square_1$

    Four or five times a week
    $\square_2$

    Two or three times a week
    $\square_3$

Two to four times a month
$\square_4$

One time a month or less
$\square_5$

Never
$\square_0$

The codes are the numbers to the right and just below the response boxes. You use statistical programs to tell you how many people who answered 0 to Question 1 also answered 1 to Question 8. To do this, the computer must be told the *name* of the variables (Question 4 = SEX and Question 8 = QFDRINK) *and* their *values* (0 = male and 1 = female and 1= daily or almost daily to 0 = never).

The "words" in brackets (SEX and QFDRINK) correspond to the variables represented by each question. All *code books* contain descriptions of the questions, codes, and variables associated with a survey. The code book must be assembled for the analysis. Look at this excerpt from the code book for the CARPS.

Example: Excerpt From the Code Book for the CARPS, a Survey to Detect Binge Drinking

Variable Name	Variable Label	Values: Labels and Codes
PROJID	Project code	7-digit ID
AGE	Age	Date of birth: Mo/day/year
GENDER	Gender	Gender of respondent: 0 = male; 1 = female; leave blank if missing
CNTRY	Country born in	Country person is born in: 01 = Argentina; 02 = Bolivia; 03 = Chile; 04 = Colombia; 05 = Cuba; 06 = Ecuador; 07 = El Salvador; 08 = Guatemala; 09 = Honduras; 10 = Mexico; 11 Nicaragua; 12 = Peru; 13 = Puerto Rico. Leave blank if no data
FGUILT	Frequency of feeling guilty or sorry because of drinking	1 = daily or almost daily; 2 = at least once a week, but less than daily; 3 = at least once a month, but less than weekly; 4 = less than once a month; 0 = never; Leave blank if no data
DRIVE	Drinks and drives	1 = 20 or more days in the past 12 months; 2 = 10–19 days; 3 = 6–9 days; 4 = 3–5 days; 5 = 1–2 days; 0 = never; Leave blank if no data

All variables are broken down to discrete units called values, which correspond to the codes for that variable. For instance, the frequency with which a person feels guilty or sorry for something he or she did because of alcohol use has five values: 4 = daily or almost daily; 3 = at least once a week, but less than daily; 2 = at least once a month, but less than weekly;

1 = less than once a month; 0 = never; leave blank if no data. The codes are 4, 3, 2, 1, and 0. If no information from the respondent is available, nothing is filled in.

Although statistical programs vary in terminology, they are fairly consistent in requiring variables to be named in capital letters (PROJID or GENDER) and to avoid the use of special characters such as commas or semicolons. Some programs have limits on the number of characters (usually about eight) that you can use. Variable labels are the actual name of the variable (e.g., frequency of feeling guilty or sorry is the actual name of the variable named FGUILT). To understand your data, the computer needs to know the names of the variables such as (FGUILT), the variable labels (frequency of feeling guilty or sorry), and value labels and values (daily or almost daily = 1; at least once a week but less than daily = 2, etc.). (Please note: Your statistical program may use slightly different terms, but the idea will be exactly the same.)

In large survey projects, the code book is the project's official record. The code book contains the survey instrument; variable names, labels, and values or codes; survey methods, characteristics; findings; and the survey instrument (including scoring system, if relevant) and survey team members. If you or any of your colleagues and associates ever want to use the data from the survey (say, to do additional analyses) or repeat the survey (say, on a different sample), you will find the code book to be essential. Because of their detail, this type of code book is sometimes referred to as an operations manual.

Sample code books in their entirety can be found on the Web. To find them, go to your favorite search engine and enter "surveys AND code book" or +survey+codebook.

Establishing Reliable Coding

To ensure reliable data in small surveys—say, with just one person doing the coding—you should recode all or a sample of the data to check for consistency. The second coding should take place about a week after the first coding. This is enough time for the coder to forget the first set of codes so that they are not just automatically reproduced. After the data are coded a second time, the two sets of codes should be compared.

In large or very large surveys, a second person should independently code a sample of the data. To ensure reliability between coders, provide definitions of all terms and formally train all coders.

Despite your best efforts at setting up a high-quality code book and data management system, the coders may not always agree with one another. To find out about the extent of their agreement—intercoder or interrater reliability—you can calculate a statistic called *kappa*. Kappa measures how much better than chance the agreement is between a pair of coders. Here is the principle behind the kappa.

Measuring Agreement: The Kappa

Suppose two reviewers are asked to independently review 100 interviews with members of a community who are about to vote on whether or not they want a new mall to be built. The reviewers are to study the transcripts of the interviews to find how many people mention displacement of single-owner stores by national chains during the discussion. The reviewers are asked to code 1 for "no" if a person does not mention displacement at least once and 2 for "yes" if he or she does mention displacement. Here are the reviewers' codes:

Reviewer 1

Reviewer 2	No	Yes	
No	20[c]	15	35[b]
Yes	10	55[d]	65
	30[a]	70	

Reviewer 1 says that 30 (a) of the 100 interviews do not contain reference to displacement of single-owner stores, whereas Reviewer 2 says that 35 (b) do not. The two reviewers agree that 20 (c) studies do not include mention of displacement.

What is the best way to describe the extent of agreement between the reviewers? 20 of 100 or 20% (c) is probably too low because the reviewers also agree that 55% (d) of studies include mention of displacement. The total agreement: 55% + 20% is an overestimate because with only two categories (yes and no), some agreement may occur by chance.

This is shown in the following formula in which O is the observed agreement and C is the chance agreement.

Measuring Agreement between Two Coders: The *Kappa* (κ) Statistic

$\kappa = O - C$ (Agreement beyond chance)

$1 - C$ (Agreement possible beyond chance)

Here is how the formula works with the preceding example.

1. Calculate how many interviews the reviewers may agree by chance DO NOT include mention of displacement of small stores. This is done by multiplying the number of nos and dividing by 100 because there are 100 interviews: $30 \times 35/100 = 10.5$

2. Calculate how many interviews they may agree by chance DO include mention of displacement by multiplying the number of interviews that each reviewer found to include mention. This is done by multiplying the number of yeses and dividing by 100: $70 \times 65/100 = 40.5$

3. Add the two numbers obtained in Steps 1 and 2 and divide by 100 to get a proportion for *chance agreement:* $(10.5 + 45.5)/100 = 0.56$.

The *observed agreement* is 20% + 55% = 75% or 0.75. Therefore the agreement beyond chance is $0.75 - 0.56 = 0.19$: the numerator.

The *agreement possible beyond chance* is 100% minus the chance agreement of 56% or $1 - 0.56 = 0.44$: the denominator.

$$\kappa = \frac{0.19}{0.44}$$

$$\kappa = 0.43$$

What is a "high" kappa? Some experts have attached the following qualitative terms to kappas: 0.0 0 – 0.20 = slight; 0.20 – 0.40 = fair; 0.40 – 0.60 = moderate; 0.60 – 0.80 = substantial and 0.80 – 0.10 = almost perfect.

How do you achieve substantial or almost perfect agreement—reliability—among reviewers? You do this by making certain that all reviewers collect and record data on exactly the same topics and that they agree in advance on what each important variable means. The "fair" kappa of 0.43 obtained by the reviewers above can be due to differences between the reviewers' and surveyors' definitions, poor training in the use of the definitions, and mistakes in coding.

Reviewing Surveys for Missing Data

Missing data result from unanswered questions or lost surveys. You should review the first completed surveys as soon as you receive them, before you enter any data. In self-administered, written surveys, especially mailed questionnaires, expect to find unanswered questions. Respondents may not answer questions because they do not want to, they miss the questions (do not see them), or they do not understand them. People may not understand the directions for completing the survey or the questions because the amount of reading is too great or the reading level is too high. Respondents may be unsure of how to respond (completely fill in the boxes, circle the correct answer, etc.). They may find the format difficult to use.

Confusing question formats lead to missing data because respondents do not know how to answer the question. Extensive cognitive pretests and pilot testing may overcome some problems that cause respondents to misunderstand survey questions. Cognitive pretests are interviews with potential respondents that ask them to interpret each question and response. Pilot tests are tests of the survey in the planned survey setting. These two activities will tell you before you go to the field that a particular format is unusable or some questions do not make sense. But no matter what you do, you can expect some missing data: That is a sure thing!

A major problem faced by surveyors is how to handle missing data. Say, you mail 100 surveys and get 95 back. You proudly announce that you have a 95% response rate. After closer examination, you discover that half the respondents did not answer Question 5, and that not one of the 25 survey questions was completed by every respondent. With all that missing information, you cannot really claim to have a 95% response rate for all questions.

What should be done about missing responses? In some cases, you may be able to go back to the respondents and ask them to answer the questions they omitted. In small surveys, where the respondents are known—say, in an office setting or within a school—the respondents may be easily contacted. But collecting information a second time is usually impractical, if not impossible, in most surveys. Some surveys are anonymous, and you do not even know who the respondents are. In institutional settings, you may have to go back to the Institutional Review Board to get permission to contact the respondents a second time. This may take time and delay your survey's completion.

Computerized surveys can be programmed so that the respondent must answer one question before proceeding to the next. Some respondents may find this approach frustrating, however, and refuse to complete the survey. Although compelling respondents to answer all questions is touted as a major advantage of online and other computer-based surveys, some surveyors think that forcing respondents to answer every question is coercive and unethical. These surveyors argue that in many surveys, participation is voluntary; respondents can quit when they want. A computer program that forces people to answer a question even if they prefer not to may be construed by some people as violating the ethical principle of autonomy or respect for individuals. Moreover, the survey may result in unreliable information because some people may enter a meaningless answer just to be able to move on to the next question.

Entering the Data

Data entry is the process of getting the survey's responses into the computer. It usually takes three forms. In the first, data from a coded survey are entered into a database management program or spreadsheet. The data are then saved in text or ASCII files so that they can be exported into a statistical program such as SPSS, SAS, or Stata. A second type of data entry involves entering data directly into a statistical program such as SPSS, SAS, or Stata. In the third form of data entry, the respondent or interviewer enters responses directly into the computer. Data entry of this type is associated with computer-assisted interviewing, online surveys, and scanned surveys. The responses are automatically entered into database management systems or statistical programs (usually through special translation software). Programs are also available that will automatically convert one file format into another (say, from SAS to Stata).

Each data entry, database management, and statistical program has its own conventions and terminology. Some programs will tell you that when entering data you are setting up "records" for each respondent. The record consists of the person's unique ID (identification code) and the person's "observations" (response choices, scores, comments, etc.). Other programs consider the unit of analysis (such as the person) as the observation, and the data collected on each observation as the variables or fields. The example that follows is a simple data set for six people.

Example: Survey Responses From Six People

Respid	Gender	Married	Children	Binge	Guilt
1	1	3	2	1	1
2	2	4	1	3	2
3	2	3	2	3	2
4	1	3	2	1	2
5	1	1	1	1	2
6	1	3	1	3	1

In this example, the table is organized so that the rows are for each person, and the columns are their data. That is, Person 2's data are 2, 4, 1, 3, and 2. Many statistical programs will require you to tell the computer where on the data line a variable is located. For instance, in the example, the person's gender is called GENDER, and data on gender can be found in Column 2. Binge drinking is called BINGE, and the data for this variable can be found in Column 5.

Database management programs, statistical programs, and computer-assisted surveys with automatic data entry can facilitate accuracy by being programmed to allow the entry of only legal codes. For instance, if the codes should be entered as 001 – 010, then you can write rules so that an entry of 01 or 10 is not permitted. If you try to enter 01 or 10, you will get an error message. With minimum programming, the program can also check each entry to ensure that it is consistent with previously entered data and that skip patterns are respected. That is, the program can make sure that the fields for questions that are to be skipped by some respondents are coded as skips and not as missing data. Designing a computer-assisted protocol requires skill and time. No protocol should be regarded as error free until it has been tested and retested in the field.

Cleaning the Data

Once the data are entered, they need to be cleaned. A clean data set can be used by anyone to get the same results you do when you run the analysis. Data become "dirty" for a number of reasons including miscoding, incorrect data entry, and missing responses.

One good way to avoid dirty data is to rely on scanned or online surveys. If you enter data by hand, however, make sure that coders or data enterers are experienced, well trained, and supervised.

Run frequencies on your data as soon as you have about 10% of the responses in. Run them again and again until you are sure that the survey is running smoothly. Frequencies are tabulations of the responses to each survey question. If your data set is relatively small, you can visually scan the frequencies for errors. For large databases with many tables or records, variables, skip patterns, and open-ended text responses, you may need to do a systematic computerized check. All leading statistical programs provide for cleaning specifications that can be used during data entry and later as a separate cleaning process.

Several other problems may require you to clean up the data. These include having to deal with the complete absence of data because some surveys have not been returned, with missing data from surveys that have been returned, and with surveys that contain data that are very different form the average respondents.

To minimize low response rates, make sure the survey is meaningful to the intended responders. Is the topic important enough so that they feel compelled to answer the questions? Be sure to prove to the respondent that you will respect the rules of confidentiality. Check the survey's readability level, format, and aptness of the language through cognitive pretesting and scientific translation. If the reading level is too high, the format is cluttered, or the translation is poor, then you can count on people to ignore the survey. If you are conducting an interview, spend the time and money to train and monitor interviewers. You can lose people if they do not understand or like the survey or interviewer. It often helps to offer financial or other incentives (such as gifts or gift certificates) to encourage respondents to respond.

PRESENTING THE SURVEY RESULTS

OVERVIEW

Survey results can be shown on the survey form itself and in tables, graphs, diagrams, or pictures. Survey reports often include summary tables. Their purpose is to describe respondents and show relationships and changes. Follow the rules if you plan to use tables. For example, use the table's columns to show the independent variables such as group and timing of survey (baseline, six months later, and three years later). Select a table format and use it consistently, rely on vertical lines sparingly, and present data in logical order such as from most to least frequent.

Pie diagrams show the proportion occupied by each response category. Each slice of the pie must be equal in proportion to the number or percentage of responses it represents. Bar graphs are commonly used to display survey data because they provide an overview of several kinds of information—comparisons and changes—at one glance. Line graphs also show changes and differences in groups. Be careful not to oversell and make a one-point change in score look significant unless it really is.

Many surveys result in written reports. Consider including these sections in yours: Abstract, summary, table of contents and figures, glossary of terms, statement of purposes or objectives, methods, results, conclusions, recommendations, references, index, appendix, and acknowledgments.

Computerized presentations are often used to describe survey findings. You can follow simple rules to design your presentation. Special attention should be paid to how you deliver a presentation so that people can follow your talk. Computerized presentations are a good choice if you plan to make last-minute changes and if you want immediate feedback from the audience.

REPRODUCING THE QUESTIONNAIRE

Survey results can be shown on the survey form itself, in tables, graphs, diagrams, or pictures. Set the responses off in some way. Look at this:

Example: Reporting Results With the Questionnaire

3. In the *past four weeks,* how much of the time have you felt depressed?

Check one box

☐	All of the time	5%
☐	Most of the time	3%
☐	A good bit of the time	8%
☐	Some of the time	42%
☐	A little of the time	32%
☐	None of the time	10%

The advantage of using the survey form to give results is to let the reader or listener see the questions and response choices. This approach shows the survey's raw data. It provides the data without any analysis or interpretation.

USING TABLES

Survey reports nearly always have tables. Their purpose is to describe respondents and show relationships and changes. Look at these shell tables:

Example: Shell Table Describing Children in Two Schools

	School 1	School 2
Characteristic	*n (%)*	*n (%)*
Age in years	____	____
Grade point average	____	____
Reading scores	____	____
Mathematics scores	____	____
Science scores	____	____

Example: Shell Table for Comparing Children in Two Schools

	School 1	School 2		
Characteristic	*n (%)*	*n (%)*	*t*	*p*
Age in years	____	____	____	____
Grade point average	____	____	____	____
Reading scores	____	____	____	____
Mathematics scores	____	____	____	____
Science scores	____	____	____	____

The first table provides the format for listing the percentage of children in two schools who

have certain characteristics (such as age and grade point average). The second table will let you put in statistics used to test if the differences are meaningful.

Table 7.1 is another example that shows statistically significant differences (indicated by one and two asterisks). This table also has a source listed: The National Children's Health Survey, Center for Health Statistics. Include the source of the information when it is not obvious. The source is not obvious if it comes from anyone but the reporter. Notice, too, that the scores are explained in superscript note a.

Table 7.1   Children with Healthy and Unhealthy Lifestyles[a] in Four Schools

	Healthy	Unhealthy
Schools	*N (%)*	*(N%)*
Alameda	140 (19)	123 (17)
Berkeley (*N* = 152)	100 (14)	52* (7)
Delacorte (*N* = 227)	89 (12)	138** (18)
Santa Inez (*N* = 91)	45 (6)	46 (7)
Total (*N* = 374)	374	359

SOURCE: Self-Administered Survey administered by The National Children's Health Survey, Center for Health Statistics.

a. Scores of 75 to 100 indicate healthy lifestyles. Scores of 26 to 74 indicate neither healthy nor unhealthy lifestyles. Scores of 1 to 25 indicate unhealthy lifestyles.

*p = .003 between healthy and unhealthy within school; **p = .002 between healthy and unhealthy within school.

Look at Tables 7.2 and 7.3:

Table 7.2   Changes in Self-Efficacy (in percentages)

	Under 65 Years		65 Years and Older	
	2004	*2005*	*2004*	*2005*
Level	*(n = 128)*	*(n = 49)*	*(n = 104)*	*(n = 212)*
High	0	70	0	69
Medium	57	28	57	31
Low	43	2	43	0

SOURCE: *The Self-Efficacy Scale* (New York: National Press).

NOTE: Scale is 1 to 9, with scores of 1 to 3 = high; scores of 7 to 9 = low.

Table 7.3 Changes in Self-Efficacy (in percentages)

Level	2004		2005	
	Under 65 Years (n = 128)	65 Years and Older (n = 104)	Under 65 Years (n = 49)	65 Years and Older (n = 212)
High	0	0	70	69
Medium	57	57	28	31
Low	43	43	2	0

SOURCE: *The Self-Efficacy Scale* (New York: National Press).

NOTE: Scale is 1 to 9, with scores of 1 to 3 = high; scores of 7 to 9 = low.

Which tells you more: Table 7.2 or Table 7.3? If the emphasis of the survey is on changes between groups (under 65 years versus 65 years and older), then Table 7.2 is better. If you want to emphasize the changes that took place over a one-year time period, then Table 7.3 is better.

Some Table Preparation Rules

1. Tables display columns and rows of numbers, percentages, scores, and statistical test results. Decide how many columns and rows you can include and still keep the table readable.

2. Each table should have a title that summarizes its purpose and content.

3. When the source of a table's data is not immediately obvious, it should be given.

4. When you use a term that may be confusing, define it. Set off definitions with asterisks or superscript letters.

5. Columns are the independent variables such as group and timing of survey (baseline, six months later, and three years later).

6. Select a table format and use it consistently. The tables in the previous examples use captions in which the first letter of each word (except prepositions and articles) in the

columns is capitalized. In the rows, only the first word is capitalized. Many people use only horizontal lines in tables. Use vertical lines sparingly especially if you also use horizontal lines.

7. Present data in some logical order. One commonly used order is from most frequent to least frequent, although the reverse may be appropriate, too. This idea is to be logical so that the reader can follow.

8. Include the sample size and differentiate between numbers, percentages, and other statistics.

All word processing programs can help you format tables so that they are easy to read. If you use tables frequently, learn how to use your program's table functions.

DRAWING PIE DIAGRAMS

Pie diagrams show visually the proportion of the whole that each response category occupies. Suppose you were conducting a survey of 80 library users' needs and wanted to distinguish the needs of people of different ages. Suppose also that you found that 40 respondents were relatively young—say, between 18 and 25 years of age—and only 10 were between 25 and 35 with the remaining 30 people over 45. You can describe your findings effectively by presenting them this way:

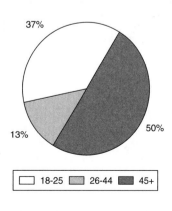

Figure 7.1 Library Users: *N* = 80

Look at this:

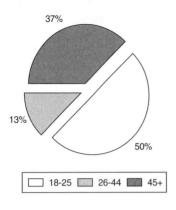

Figure 7.2   Library Users: *N* = 80

This pie chart has the same proportion of users as previously. By cutting the pie, you emphasize the different sizes of each slice.

If you plan to use pie diagrams frequently, you can rely on graphics programs. Spreadsheet, word processing, and other programs include graphics functions that enable you to draw pies from tables of data. The key to an accurate pie diagram is its scale. Each slice must be equal in proportion to the number or percentage of responses it represents. 50% of responses is half the pie, 25% is one quarter and so on. Remember to keep the slices to no more than about six, or the pie will be too cluttered.

USING BAR GRAPHS

Bar graphs are commonly used to display survey data because they provide an overview of several kinds of information at one glance. Look at Figure 7.3, a graph of changes in behavior between boys and girls from 1985 to 2005.

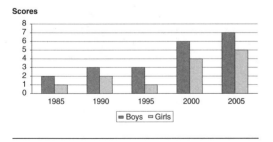

Figure 7.3   Boys' and Girls' Behavior Survey

This graph tells you two things at once:

- Boys' and girls' behavior changed over time.
- Boys had consistently higher scores than girls.

Now look at Figure 7.4.

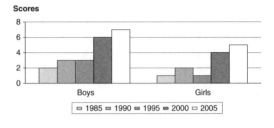

Figure 7.4   Boys' and Girls' Behavior Survey

This graph of the same information concentrates on boys and girls, although you still get two kinds of information at one glance.

Figure 7.5 is a graph of the same information focusing on scores, and you can see two kinds of data at once.

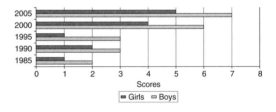

Figure 7.5   Boys' and Girls' Behavior Survey

Bar graphs should always have a title, a legend or key to the bars, and any other explanations needed to keep the results honest. Remember that seeing can be deceiving. Just because the graph suggests differences does not mean they are real (significant and practical).

Figure 7.6 shows the same data presented in a line graph. Line graphs are better than bars at showing the flow of change over time. Most graphics programs will allow you to automatically switch from one type of graph to another so that you can actually see which one best describes your survey data. The objective is accuracy.

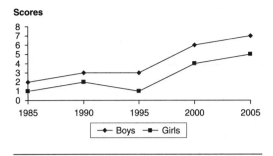

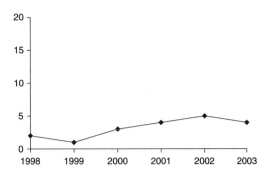

Figure 7.6   Boys' and Girls' Behavior Survey

Using Line Graphs

Line graphs are drawings that allow you to show changes and compare groups. Be careful not to oversell and make a 1-point change in a score look significant unless it really is. Look at these scores:

Score	Number of Respondents With Score
1	2
2	1
3	3
4	4
5	5
6	4
Total	19

Here are two graphs, each of which has been plotted as a line graph to represent the scores and their frequency (number).

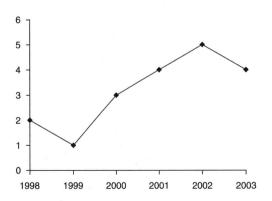

Which graph is more accurate? The first graph is the computer's choice. The graph below it is not. In the second graph, the difference in scores certainly looks less impressive.

Which is preferred bar or line graph? If in doubt, experiment. To show comparisons, tables and bar charts seem to work best. For changes over time, line graphs win.

Drawing Diagrams or Pictures

Use pictures or diagrams to get your point across. Suppose you want to describe your survey's research design. Compare the words with the diagram.

Example: Words and Diagrams in Survey Reports

We used a design in which schools were the sampling units. Fourteen schools with 2,000 total students were eligible to participate in an injury prevention program. We randomly selected 10 schools with a total of 945 students. Five schools with a total of 443 students were randomly assigned to receive the curriculum. Of the five schools who received the curriculum, 425 students completed the baseline survey. Of the 502 students not receiving the curriculum, 450 completed the baseline survey. We obtained 12-month follow-up data on 400 students in the five schools receiving the curriculum. One school not receiving the curriculum dropped out, and we collected 12-month follow-up survey data in the remaining four schools on 213 students.

Now look at this:

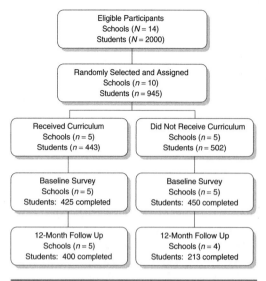

A diagram like this is very helpful in explaining complex research designs. The diagram relies on the principles used to make an organizational or flow chart.

All main word processing programs and spreadsheets have functions that allow you to easily convert a table of data into a chart. If you use flow charts often, you should consider buying a graphics program.

WRITING THE RESULTS OF A SURVEY

A fairly typical conclusion to a survey's activities is a written report of its purposes, methods, results, conclusions, and recommendations. One question always seems to come up when you sit down to organize the report: How detailed and technical should you be? If you are too technical, you may reduce your readership substantially; on the other hand, ignoring the technical details may subject your report to criticism.

Three aims should guide your writing.

- Be comprehensive.
- Organize carefully.
- Write as clearly as you can.

Sound like one of your earliest school teachers warning you about a book report? Perhaps. But

if these three criteria are applied, your report is more likely to be read than otherwise.

Aiming for comprehensiveness means including as much as possible so that anyone who wants to can understand the report. You must organize the report so that anyone can find out what he or she wants to know. If I am interested in why you choose the XYZ Self-Efficacy Survey, I should be able to find that information easily. Writing clearly is always a desirable aim. In survey reports, clarity means using standard language conventions and making sure that all ambiguous terms are defined.

Organizing the Report

Consider including all these:

Abstract

Summary

Table of contents

Table of tables and figures

Glossary of terms

Road map: What to look for in the report and where to find it

Statement of purposes or objectives

Methods

Results

Conclusions

Recommendations

References

Index

Appendix

Acknowledgments

Abstract. The abstract is usually about 150 to 250 words. Consider using a structured abstract. Look at this:

Example: Structured Abstract of a Survey Report

Purpose: To identify community attitudes toward integrating boys and men into Women Forward (WF), a traditionally all-female grassroots organization aimed at encourage girls and women to enter politics.

Research design: A cross-sectional survey of 150 people

Survey: 15-minute telephone interviews conducted during July 2004

Respondents: An 82% response rate was obtained. Of the respondents, 70% were men, and 62% of respondents were 35 years of age or younger. Respondents were randomly selected from local political organizations.

Main outcome: Support for integration

Results: Eighty-four men (97.6%) and 32 women (86%) supported integration. These differences are not significant. Respondents 35 years of age and under are significantly less eager than older respondents ($p = .04$) to integrate men into WF.

Conclusions: Although men and women are about equal in their support of integrating men into WF, younger respondents—regardless of gender—are less enthusiastic. Interpret these findings cautiously because 70% of respondents were male.

This abstract has 152 words, counting the headings. Your word processing program is likely to have a function for counting words.

Summary. The summary is a distillation of all the report's key components (objectives, methods, findings). It should be about three pages long and take five minutes to read. You can provide more detail than you do in the abstract and add information on who conducted the survey. You can also include one or two important tables or figures.

Table of Contents. The table of contents should list all major sections of the report with the associated page numbers.

List of Tables and Figures. List each table and figure and give its complete name and the page number on which it appears. In some reports, tables and figures go at the end in a separate section.

Glossary of Terms. All technical terms (e.g., random sampling), abbreviations (e.g., CBS = Center for Business and Science), and ambiguous concepts (e.g., healthy, smart, hostile) can be included in the glossary.

Road Map: What to Look for in the Report and Where to Find It. Some reports are complex, and the reader needs a road map to follow it. For instance, suppose your report has two major components: Part 1 and Part 2. Tell the reader how to find each part (Separately bound? Click on a word? An icon?). Tell what is in each (i.e., Part 1 has a description of the survey project, Part 2 discusses the validation).

Purposes. The purposes are the survey's objectives. Discuss in the report why you did the survey. Did you do the survey to find out how satisfied participants are with their benefits? To find out which benefits will satisfy them?

Outcomes. On which main dependent variables or outcomes does the survey focus? These may be changes in knowledge, attitudes, behavior, health, quality of life.

Methods. What was done? With whom? Was the effort worthwhile? To answer these questions, discuss the following:

- The type of survey (a self-administered questionnaire, telephone interview, etc.) and the limitations that resulted because you chose that type of survey: For example, suppose that in a telephone survey of the elderly, about 5% of eligible persons do not have access to telephones. The frailest and poorest persons will be underrepresented. Ask: What does this mean for the conclusions?
- Survey questions asked: Give examples; include the survey in the appendix if you cannot include it in the text.
- Survey logistics: During which months, over what period of time, and how frequently was the survey administered? By whom was it administered? How were the administrators trained? How was the quality of the administration monitored? What are the limitations that resulted? For example, say you trained five people, but one was not adequate. What might this have done to the results?
- Survey construction: Give the origin of questions, describe pilot testing, and discuss reliability and validity. Discuss the limitations that

resulted during construction. For example, the validation study may reveal that the survey is not useful with people who do not read English or Spanish at the ninth grade level.

- Sampling and response rate: What were the eligibility criteria? How did you calculate the response rate? How adequate was the response rate? Did you use incentives? Discuss the limitations. Because you did not get sufficient numbers of eligible respondents, what did this do to the results? For example, suppose you wanted half men and half women, but respondents were primarily female?
- Survey research design and its limitations: For example, suppose your survey used comparison groups that were not randomly constituted; what types of selection bias can you anticipate? How seriously does this affect your findings?
- Analysis: For each main survey outcome of interest, describe the analysis method.
- Ethics: Were respondents informed? How was confidentiality maintained?

Results. Concerning each outcome of interest, what did you find? Usually these are given as statistics.

Conclusions. What do the findings mean?

Recommendations. What do you recommend, based on the data? Warning: Not every situation warrants recommendations. Some people who commission surveys just require the data; they will themselves make the recommendations.

References. Cite those you have used in the text. Put the references in alphabetical order or list them in the order in which they appear in your text.

Index. Include an index only in very long reports.

Appendix. Include any relevant material that is too cumbersome to be contained in the report. This may mean putting a long survey in the appendix rather than in the body of the report. As a rule of thumb, 15 questions or fewer can be included in the report. Keep in mind that some single questions can have 15 choices, and these might have to be put into the appendix. For example: In the past 12 months, have you had any one of the following health problems: Headaches, stomachaches, sprained ankle or wrist, cold? Each choice is similar to a single question: In the past 12 months, have you had headaches? Have you had stomachaches? Have you had a sprained ankle or wrist? Have you had a cold?

Clear Writing

Here are some tips on clarity of items.

1. Use the active voice whenever possible.

> *Poor:* The report *is* relatively simple and *is* obviously written for the nonexpert, for there *are* very few statistical tables given. (Twenty words; three are forms of the verb "to be.")

> *Better:* The relatively simple report *is* obviously written for the nonexpert, for it *gives* very few statistical tables. (Seventeen words, two verbs)

Avoid "there is" and "there are."

> *Poor:* There are very few statistical tables in the report.

> *Better:* The report has very few statistical tables.

2. Do not sprinkle sentences with prepositional phrases. When possible, avoid: "in order to give a reason," and replace it with "to give a reason." Convert a prepositional phrase to a participle: "In the effort to get reliable attitude measures" can become, "trying to get reliable attitude measures." Convert a prepositional phrase to an adjective: "It is a question of importance" can become "It is an important question."

Replace	With
at an early date	soon
at the present time	now
in order to	to
prior to	before
subsequent to	after

Nearly all word processing programs have a grammar function. They are excellent in pointing out passive sentences. They also provide alternatives and can remind you of the grammar you may have forgotten. However, they are not perfect, and they are not interested in style.

3. Try a readability formula. Readability testing predicts the grade level of written material. Many people feel comfortable reading below grade level, but people will ignore material that is above it. All major word processing programs will give you readability statistics for some or all of your report.

This is a simple formula that gives you a good idea of how to estimate readability. The result of using the formula is called the FOG index:

1. Take a 100-word sample of your survey report.
2. Compute the average number of words per sentence. If the final sentence in your sample runs beyond 100 words, use the total number of words at the end of that sentence to compute the average.
3. Count the number of words with more than two syllables in the 100-word sample. Do not count proper nouns or three-syllable word forms ending in -ed or -es.
4. Add the average number of words per sentence to the number of words containing more than two syllables and multiply the sum by 0.4.

Suppose a 100-word passage contains an average of 20 words per sentence and 10 words of more than two syllables. The sum of these is 30. Multiplying 30 by 0.4 gives a FOG index of 12th grade.

Look at the structured abstract found earlier in this chapter. The readability statistics suggest that the abstract is of average difficulty requiring a reading level from 8th to 10th grade. Most readability formulas only look at words; they do not include numbers. If you are talking to a lay audience, keep numbers simple. Use 76% or 76.2% rather than 76.17%.

THE ORAL PRESENTATION

Oral presentations follow many of the rules of written reports. Speak clearly and slowly and pace your presentation to the audience's needs. You must be selective in oral reporting—often, a difficult task. Make sure you give audiences useful results. The board members want to know

the bottom line while the theorists want to know about validity. Lay audiences are primarily concerned with findings and participants. If you have time, you can tell them about the survey's methods and limits. All audiences expect examples of the survey questions.

COMPUTERIZED "SLIDE" PRESENTATIONS

Use the following guidelines to prepare slides.

Guidelines for Preparing Slides

- Limit each slide to one main concept.

Poor:

> **Helping School Children
> Cope With Violence**
> - Symptoms of depression
> - Symptoms of trauma
>
> **Settings for Treatment**
> - Home
> - School
> - Clinic
> - Other medical settings

Better:

> **Helping School Children
> Cope With Violence**
> - Symptoms of depression
> - Symptoms of trauma

> **Settings for Treatment**
> - Home
> - School
> - Clinic
> - Other medical settings

- Allow the listener one to two minutes per slide. The exception to this is when you have similar slides in a sequence, such as lists, pies, or graphs.
- If you adapt information from a textbook or other survey, check to see if it needs to be simplified. Check the copyright rules.
- Use no more than eight lines of text per slide and no more than six or seven words per line. The maximum is about ten words per idea. Do not expect the listener to also be a reader.

Poor:

The Poll Tax Riot

✓ About 200,000 people marched to Trafalgar Square in London as part of a nationwide campaign against a new tax system called the poll tax.

✓ The demonstration began peacefully but become one of the largest riots in 100 years.

✓ The survey team participated in the crowd as demonstrators and used this role to record semistructured interviews and the soundtrack of the demonstration on a hand-held tape recorder.

Better:

The Poll Tax Riot

✓ 200,000 people marched in Trafalgar Square

✓ Was one of largest riots in 100 years

✓ Purpose was to protest new tax

✓ Demonstration began peacefully

Survey Methods

✓ Semistructured *interviews* with demonstrators

✓ Hand-held *tape recorder* to capture "soundtrack"

- To emphasize points, underline titles, use bullets or check marks, number each point, or use contrasting colors to separate points.
- Be consistent in the use of sentences or phrases.

Poor:

How Would You Characterize a True Experiment?

- Comparing one or more groups
- It has an intervention
- Random selection
- You randomly assign people to groups

Comment: The first bullet is followed by a phrase beginning with a gerund ("ing'), whereas the second is followed by a sentence. The third bullet is a phrase, and the fourth is a sentence. This mixture is confusing to listeners.

Better:

How Would You Characterize a True Experiment?

- One or more groups are compared
- Groups receive an intervention
- Participants are randomly selected
- Participants are randomly assigned to groups

All the items in this slide are expressed as sentences.

- If you have "down time" with no appropriate slides, use a filler. These often consist of an opaque, blank slide or the title of the presentation. Do not use cartoons as the filler because they are distracting in the middle of a talk. (If you use cartoons to lighten the presentation, make sure the audience can see the caption. Also make certain no copyright restrictions or fees for use apply.)
- Use handouts to summarize information and provide technical details and references. Make sure that your name, the name of the presentation, and the date are on each page of the handout. Do not distribute handouts until you are finished speaking unless you refer to them during your talk.
- In general, upper- and lowercase letters are easier to read than all uppercase.
- Round numbers to the nearest whole number. Try to avoid decimals, but if you must, round to the nearest tenth (32.6%, *not* 32.62%).
- Limit tables to five rows and six columns.
- If graphs are used, make sure that both the X and the Y axes are clearly labeled.
- Make sure that all information on the screen is discussed in the talk.
- Be careful not to overwhelm the listener with animation, graphics, and sound. **Warning!** Do not assume you can routinely download graphics or other material from the Web. A great deal of accessible information is copyrighted.
- Use no more than four colors per slide. If you are unsure of the colors to use, consider using the program's preselected slide presentation colors. Yellow or white letters on royal blue are easy to see and read.
- Review the slides before you talk. Make sure the fonts are readable and consistent. Don't mix fonts on the same slide unless you are using the mixture to emphasize words. If possible, have someone else review the slides for content and format.

ORAL VERSUS WRITTEN REPORTS:
A DIFFERENCE IN CONVERSATION

Oral reports and written reports are different in at least one very important way. Oral reports depend on your ability to speak the details. Written reports rely on prose and pictures to speak for you. Compare these two:

Example: Tables Used in a Written and an Oral Report

Written Report

Baseline and Follow-up Mean Scores ($\overline{X}$) and Standard Deviation (*SD*)

Survey Outcome	Experimental Schools (n = 467 students)		Control Schools (n = 400 students)		Net Difference	t	p
	Baseline	*Follow-up*	*Baseline*	*Follow-up*			
	$\overline{X}$ (SD)	$\overline{X}$ (SD)	$\overline{X}$ (SD)	$\overline{X}$ (SD)			
Moral values	75.6 (11.8)	85.5 (8.8)	78.8 (10.9)	81.2 (9.6)	7.5	8.9	.0001
Religious beliefs	3.5 (0.7)	3.8 (0.7)	3.7 (0.7)	3.8 (0.7)	.19	4.7	.0001
Social responsibility	3.7 (0.7)	3.9 (0.7)	3.7 (0.7)	3.8 (0.7)	.10	2.2	.003
Ethical behavior	1.5 (2.5)	1.3 (2.3)	1.0 (2.0)	1.3 (2.4)	−.48	2.8	.06

Written Interpretation of the Table

The table gives the baseline and follow-up means and the observed net differences in scores for four survey outcomes. We used an independent *t* test to compare changes in mean scores from baseline to follow-up for the experimental and control groups. Significant differences were found favoring the experimental students in moral values, religious beliefs, and social responsibility. Differences in social responsibility approached significance, but did not reach the *p* = 0.05, the level of significance chosen for the *t* test.

Oral Report

Mean ($\overline{X}$) Differences Between Experimental (*N* = 467) And Controlschools (*N* = 400)

Outcome	Experimental $\overline{X}$		Control $\overline{X}$	
	Baseline	*Follow-Up*	*Baseline*	*Follow-Up*
Moral Values*	75.6	85.5	78.8	81.2
Religious Beliefs*	3.5	3.8	3.7	3.8
Social Responsibility*	3.7	3.9	3.7	3.8
Ethical Behavior	1.5	1.3	1.0	1.3

*Statistically different between baseline and follow-up.

Oral Interpretation. The table compares experimental and control schools. (*Point to the appropriate columns.*) We used an independent *t* test to compare the differences in mean scores from baseline to follow-up. (*Point to the appropriate rows.*) We found statistically significant differences favoring students in experimental schools in moral values, religious beliefs, and social responsibility. (*Point to the asterisks.*)

BIBLIOGRAPHY

Bates, E. S., & Abemayor, E. (1991). Slide presentation graphics using a personal computer. *Archives of Otolaryngology and Head and Neck Surgery, 117*, 1026–1030.

Braitman, L. (1991). Confidence intervals assess both clinical and statistical significance. *Annals of Internal Medicine, 114*, 515–517.

Campbell, D. T., & Stanley, J. C. (1963). *Experimental and quasi-experimental designs for research.* Chicago: Rand McNally.

Couper, M. P., Traugott, M. W., & Lamias M. J. (2001). Web survey design. *Public Opinion Quarterly, 65*, 231–253.

Dawson, B., & Trapp, R. G. (2001). *Basic and clinical biostatistics* (3rd ed.). New York: Lange Medical Books/McGraw-Hill.

Fink, A. (Ed.). (2002). *The survey kit.* Thousand Oaks, CA: Sage.

Contents of the kit:

    Fink, A. *The Survey Handbook*

    Fink, A. *How to Ask Survey Questions*

    Bourque, L. B., & Fielder, E. P. *How to Conduct Self-Administered and Mail Surveys*

    Bourque, L. B., & Fielder, E. P. *How to Conduct Telephone Surveys*

    Oishi, S. *How to Conduct In-Person Interviews for Surveys*

    Fink, A. *How to Design Survey Studies*

    Fink, A. *How to Sample in Surveys*

    Litwin, M. *How to Assess and Interpret Survey Psychometrics*

    Fink, A. *How to Manage, Analyze, and Interpret Survey Data*

    Fink, A. *How to Report on Surveys*

Fink, A. (2005). *Evaluation fundamentals: Insights into the outcomes, effectiveness, and quality of health programs* (2nd ed). Thousand Oaks, CA: Sage.

Kraemer, H. C., & Thiemann, S. (1987). *How many subjects? Statistical power analysis in research.* Thousand Oaks, CA: Sage.

Pfeiffer, W. S. (1991). *Technical writing.* New York: Macmillan.

Salkind, N. J. (2004). *Statistics for people who (think they) hate statistics* (2nd ed.). Thousand Oaks, CA: Sage.

Siegel, S. (1956). *Nonparametric statistics for the behavioral sciences.* New York: McGraw-Hill.

Spinler, S. (1991). How to prepare and deliver pharmacy presentations. *American Journal of Hospital Pharmacy, 48*, 1730–1738.

Three Web sites that can provide you with examples of surveys and lead you to find usable questions:

    www.cdc.gov

    www.field.com

    www.srl.uic.edu/Srllink/srllink.htm (This site belongs to the University of Illinois at Chicago's Survey Research Center)

INDEX

Abbreviations, 19
Abemayor, E., 103
Additive scales, 26–27
Agreement, measurement of, 87–88
Analysis of variance (ANOVA), 72, 73,
    77, 81–83
Associations, analysis of, 73–74
Averages, 78–80

Bar graphs, 91, 94
Bates, E. S., 103
Bias, 11, 19–20
Bourque, L. B., 103
Braitman, L., 103
Branching questions, 34–35

Campbell, D. T., 103
Case control designs, 59, 66–67
Categorical rating scales, 23
Category scales, 25–26
Centers for Disease Control and
    Prevention (CDC), 42
Checklist responses, 21–22
Checklists:
    question order, 34
    self-administered questionnaires, 35–36
Chi-square (χ^2), 71–72, 85
Clean data, 70, 90
Closed questions, 11, 13–15, 18–20
Cluster samples, 49–50
Codes, 15–18, 70, 85–88
Cohort designs, 59, 60, 63
Comparative rating scales, 25
Comparison group designs, 60, 64–66, 74
Computerized presentations, 91, 99–100
Computer literacy, 22
Concrete questions, 19
Concurrent validity, 31, 39
Confidence intervals, 77
Confidentiality, 32, 41–43
Construct validity, 31, 39

Content, 12–13
Content validity, 31, 39
Continuous rating scales, 24
Convenience samples, 45, 46–47, 50–51
Cookies, 42
Correlations, 69, 70–71, 81
Costs, 8, 9
Couper, M. P., 103
Credibility, 8
Cross-sectional surveys, 5, 59, 60–62

Data analysis, 6, 69–92
Data entry, 89–90
Data management, 70, 85
Dawson, B., 103
Dependent variables, 53–54, 75
Descriptive statistics, 69, 70
Design, 5–6, 59–67
Diagrams, 91, 93–96
Differences, 69, 71
Differential scales, 27–28
Dirty data, 70, 90

Effect sizes, 56–57
Eligibility criteria, 51–52
Environmental control, 59–67
Errors, 53, 76–77
Ethical issues, 41–43
Ethnicity, 43
Expert panels, 51

Fielder, E. P., 103
Fink, A., 103
Focus groups, 51
Forced-choice questions, 4
Frequency counts, 77–78
F statistic, 82, 83

Gradations, 25–26
Graphic rating scales, 24–25
Graphs, use of, 74, 91

Health Survey Foundation, 63
Hypotheses, 12–13

Independent variables, 53–54, 75
Information need, 12–13
Informed consent, 41
Instructions, 4–5
Interactive surveys, 2
Internal consistency, 39
Internet surveys.
   See Online surveys
Interval rating scales, 24
Interviews:
   cost-benefit analysis, 9
   definition, 1
   preparation process, 31, 36–37
Introductions, 32–33
Item-writing skills, 18–20

Jargon, 19

Kappa (κ) statistic, 87–88
Kraemer, H. C., 103

Lamias, M. J., 103
Language translations, 43
Length of survey, 31, 32
Like Best/Like Least (LB/LL) survey
   technique, 15–18
Line graphs, 91, 94–95
Litwin, M., 103
Longitudinal surveys, 5, 59, 60, 62–66

Mann-Whitney U test, 72, 83
McNemar test, 73
Mean, the, 78–79
Median, the, 79–80
Missing data, 70, 88–89
Mode, the, 80
Multiple-choice questions, 14
Multiple regression analysis, 71

Nonprobability samples, 45, 46–47,
   50–51
Normative survey designs, 66
Not random samples, 47
Null hypothesis, 54–55, 76

Odds, risks and, 69, 72–73
Oishi, S., 103
Online surveys, 22–23, 42–43
Open-ended questions, 4, 11, 13–18
Oral presentations, 99–101
Order of questions, 32–34
Ordinal rating scales, 23

Panel designs, 59, 60, 63–64
Pearson product-moment correlations,
   70–71, 81
Pfeiffer, W. S., 103
Pictures, 91, 95–96
Pie diagrams, 91, 93–94
Pilot tests, 6, 31–32, 37, 40
Power, 55, 56–57
Predictive validity, 31, 39
Privacy, 32, 41–43
Probability samples, 45, 46–50
p values, 77, 82–83

Quality:
   data analysis, 76
   interviews, 37
   ready-to-use surveys, 38–39
Quasi-experimental designs, 64–65
Questions:
   construction, 4, 13–18
   order of, 32–34
Question-writing skills, 20–21
Quota samples, 51

Random samples, 5, 45, 48,
   59, 60–61
Range, 81
Rank-order correlation, 70
Rating scales, 11, 23–26
Ratio rating scales, 24
Ready-to-use surveys, 38–39
Regressions, 69, 71
Relationships, analysis of, 73–74
Reliability, 7–8, 31–32, 37–40, 87–88
Responses:
   closed questions, 21–23
   formats, 34
   frequency analysis, 90
   grouping method, 78
   open-ended questions, 15–18
   response rates, 6–7, 46, 57
Results, reporting of, 7, 91–101
Risks and odds, 69, 72–73

Salkind, N. J., 103
Sample size, 46–47, 52–57, 73
Sampling, 5–6, 45–57, 59–61
Satisfaction surveys, 15–18
Scaling, 26–29
Scientific surveys, 1
Self-administered questionnaires:
   appearance, 34
   cost-benefit analysis, 9
   definition, 1
   preparation process, 31, 35–36

Shell tables, 92
Siegel, S., 103
Simple random cluster samples,
    49–50
Simple random samples, 47–50
Skip patterns, 34–35
Slide presentations.
    See Computerized presentations
Snowball samples, 51
Spearman rank-order correlation, 70
Specific need surveys, 1, 8–10
Spinler, S., 103
Standard deviation, 55–57, 81
Standard error, 53
Stanley, J. C., 103
Statistical methods, 46, 53–57, 69–90
Statistical significance, 76–77
Stratified random samples, 45, 48–49
Subgroups, 54
Summary tables, 91, 92–93, 101
Summated scales, 28–29
Survey Research Center, University of
    Illinois at Chicago, 103
Surveys:
    analytical method selection, 73–76
    basic components, 4–8
    content, 11–29
    cost-benefit analysis, 9
    definition, 1
    language translations, 43
    length, 31, 32

preparation process, 35–37
purpose, 2, 8–10
sample and design, 5–6
usefulness, 3–4, 8
Systematic samples, 45, 50, 51

Tables, 91, 92–93, 101
Tallies, 77–78
Term definitions, 12
Thiemann, S., 103
Training skills, 36
Translations, 43
Trapp. R. G., 103
Traugott, M. W., 103
Trend designs, 59, 60, 62–63
True experimental designs, 64–66
t test, 72, 73, 83–84
Type I/Type II errors, 76–77

Validity, 7–8, 31–32, 37–40
Variables, 53–54, 75
Variance, 81
Variation, 80–81

Web surveys, 22–23, 42–43
Wilcoxon rank sum.
    See Mann-Whitney U test
Writing skills, 18–22
Written reports, 91, 96–101

Yes/no responses, 21

About the Author

Arlene Fink (Ph.D.) is Professor of Medicine and Public Health at the University of California, Los Angeles. She is an evaluation and policy adviser to UCLA's Robert Wood Johnson Clinical Scholars Program and president of Arlene Fink Associates. She has conducted survey studies throughout the United States and abroad and has trained thousands of health professionals, social scientists, and educators. In addition, she has written 10 textbooks and nearly 100 monographs and articles.